SERMON
SPARKS

Other Abingdon Press Books by Thomas H. Troeger

So That All Might Know: Preaching That Engages the Whole Congregation
with H. Edward Everding Jr.

The Parable of Ten Preachers

Preaching While the Church Is Under Reconstruction

Imagining a Sermon

Trouble at the Table: Gathering the Tribes for Worship
with Carol Doran

Ten Strategies for Preaching in a Multi Media Culture

SERMON
SPARKS

122 IDEAS TO IGNITE YOUR PREACHING

Tagged by theme and lectionary passage

THOMAS H. TROEGER

Abingdon Press
Nashville

SERMON SPARKS
122 IDEAS TO IGNITE YOUR PREACHING

Copyright © 2011 by Abingdon Press

All rights reserved.

This book is printed on acid-free paper.

Library of Congress Cataloging-in-Publication Data

Troeger, Thomas H., 1945-
  Sermon sparks : 122 ideas to ignite your preaching : tagged by theme
and lectionary passage / Thomas H. Troeger.
    p. cm.
  Includes index.
  ISBN 978-1-4267-4098-5 (pbk. : alk. paper) 1. Lectionary preaching.
I. Title.
  BV4235.L43T76 2011
  251'.6—dc23

2011032923

11 12 13 14 15 16 17 18 19 20—10 9 8 7 6 5 4 3 2 1

MANUFACTURED IN THE UNITED STATES OF AMERICA

CONTENTS

Acknowledgments vii

Chapter 1 How to Use This Book 1

Chapter 2 Year A 5

Chapter 3 Year B 47

Chapter 4 Year C 89

Notes 137

Index by Biblical Passage 139

Index by Liturgical Season 143

Index by Theme, Image, and Pastoral Need 145

ACKNOWLEDGMENTS

I am indebted to David Howell, the editor and publisher of the journal *Lectionary Homiletics* (http://www.lectionary.com/search.html), for inviting me ten years ago to supply a monthly column for his publication. He wanted me to stir the homiletical imagination of preachers while highlighting some of the larger theological and pastoral themes of the Revised Common Lectionary. He also graciously consented to the gathering and publishing of these homiletical reflections in this book. Besides producing print- and Web-based publications, David Howell has sponsored major ecumenical conferences on preaching that have been attended now by thousands of clergy from all over North America. He has made a major contribution to preaching and to continuing homiletical education. Therefore, I am delighted to dedicate this book to him in a spirit of gratitude for all he has provided to enrich the ministry of the clergy and the churches, institutions, and individuals they serve.

I also want to thank Yale Divinity School for sabbatical time to gather and revise the full manuscript of this book. I give special thanks to Professor Nora Tubbs Tisdale with whom I regularly team teach homiletics. She is a colleague whose gracious way of being creates an environment where creativity can thrive. I also am grateful for the students and faculty of both the Yale Divinity School and the Institute of Sacred Music, where I share a joint appointment. Working with splendid liturgists, musicians, and dancers while creating and delivering sermons has nurtured the prayer and scholarship from which many of these homiletical reflections flow. Finally, I am as always indebted to Merle Marie, who encourages my work while she creates her own lively musings on Scripture and the work of the Spirit.

Thomas H. Troeger
Epiphany 2011

HOW TO USE THIS BOOK

A ll of these pieces are "sparks" for homilies, initial ideas to ignite a sermon in a preacher's heart and mind. They are not full-length sermons but rather brief homiletical meditations. Sometimes I reflect on a single reading, but other times I write about several interrelated passages in order to identify a theme for a season or to trace larger patterns of theological insight.

I have indexed the book so you can easily find what you need, whether you are a preacher who chooses the texts for your sermons or follows the Revised Common Lectionary. The book is user-friendly for both kinds of preachers, featuring indexes by biblical passage, by liturgical season, and by theme, image, and pastoral need.

There is one chapter for each liturgical year—A, B, and C—always starting with Advent, then moving in sequence through all the seasons. Whenever I name a proper in a subtitle before my reflection, I list only those lessons on which I comment. Not every lection is covered, and sometimes there is more than one reflection on the same passage, either because it is featured in all three years or because I know it is central to every preacher's ministry: for example, John 1:1-14 is the gospel reading for Christmas in years A, B, and C, and I give a reflection on it for each year.

If you cannot find a lection by liturgical year, check the index of biblical passages. Several are used more than once in the three-year cycle, and my reflection upon it may appear in another year. For example, John

20:1-18 is used for Easter Day in years A, B, and C, but my reflection on it appears only in Year A.

I have discovered in myself and in many other preachers that there is sometimes a tendency to develop what I call "pericopeitis": we fall into a pattern of constantly limiting our sermons to the narrow consideration of a single biblical passage. Preaching from a single text often works fine, but there are many times when a sermon cries out for the larger context of the passage or for a broader theological perspective. I have observed enough outbreaks of pericopeitis to conclude that taking care to avoid it is worthy of every preacher's attention. The cure is not to abandon preaching in depth on a particular passage, but to use the passage more creatively. Here are some remedies that I have incorporated into many of the homiletical reflections in this collection.

1. Take a key word in a text and do a word study. Trace how often and in what different ways the same biblical author uses the word. Or see how different biblical writers treat the same word. You could do the same with a key character in the text. Whether you use a word study or a character study, either will often lead to insights and illustrations that you never dreamed possible when confining your study to a single passage.

2. Rather than preaching straight from the text, examine the relationship between the text and the historical situation that it is addressing. This works especially well with letters, pronouncements, and gospel passages that are addressing new historical developments in the life of the community. The word of God emerges not simply from the text itself, but also from the dynamic relationship between pericope and the context in which and for which it was penned. This method gives us a greater sense of how God's word comes through the living transactions of language and human struggle.

3. Seek out visual depictions, hymns, poems, and prayers that build on the passage and that are effectively *midrashim* upon the pericope—that is, creative retellings of the passage. These extra-biblical resources will help you preach about the varied ways the passage has functioned in different times and places.

4. Use additional passages in the biblical book from which you are preaching. Even if your tradition expects you to preach from the assigned lessons in the Lectionary, there is no rubric against bringing in other related passages that deepen and illumine your exposition of the required biblical text.

This is just a list to get you started. The goal is to avoid developing the impression that the word of God is like stray pieces of a picture puzzle: we get another piece each week, but never the larger pattern. By avoiding pericopeitis we communicate the transforming grace that comes as we grow more and more rooted in the God in whom "we live, and move, and have our being" (Acts 17:28 KJV).

One final observation on how to use this book: in addition to the indexes by biblical passage and liturgical season, I have included an index by theme, image, and pastoral need. Sometimes a wedding, a funeral, or other pastoral occasion arises and we remember an image or idea from our reading that we want to reuse in another context but we cannot easily find it. I am providing this index to help with such a situation, and also because it will make the book user-friendly to preachers who often think by theme or image and are looking for fresh ideas to get them started.

I know from teaching homiletics for over thirty years that we preachers sometimes accumulate a pile of thoughts from our research and reading, but they have not yet taken fire as a sermon. We need an insight, a new angle, a fresh perspective—a spark!—to set our thinking ablaze. I pray that these sermon sparks ignite your heart and mind so that the Holy Spirit, the source of all faithful creativity, will kindle the light and truth of the gospel in your listeners.

CHAPTER 2

YEAR A

The Realism of Advent and Christmas

*Year A, Advent 2: Isaiah 11:1-10, Advent 3: Matthew 11:2-11,
Christmas 1 (First Sunday after Christmas Day): Matthew 2:13-23*

What does it mean to be realistic? Worldly realism knows that life is brutal, tragic, and hard. Realists know what "the bottom line" is. Realists do not get carried away by dreams or enthusiasm. Realists have been through the wars.

Worldly realism fills the lessons we read during Advent and Christmastide. International conflicts haunt the book of Isaiah, and Herod slaughters innocent children (Matthew 2:16). The Bible confirms what the world knows: life is brutal, tragic, and hard.

But side by side with these stories of oppression and violence we read about the most extravagant hopes of the human heart. The Magi follow a star. The prophet Isaiah foretells a ruler who

> won't judge by appearances
> nor decide by hearsay.
> He will judge the needy
> with righteousness,
> and decide with equity
> for those who suffer in the land. (Isaiah 11:3-4)

5

> The wolf will live with the lamb
>   and the leopard will lie down
>   with the young goat;
>   the calf and the young lion
>   will feed together,
>   and a little child will lead them. (Isaiah 11:6)

How are we to understand the contrast between the slaughter of inno-cent children and the Magi's hope-filled quest, between power politics and the prophet's visions of a transformed world? If our *only* standard of realism is that life is brutal, tragic, and hard, then we will conclude that Herod gives us realism while the Magi and the prophet give us legend and fantasy.

But what if our standard of realism is greater than the world's? What if realism means believing in the whole range of what the heart can envi-sion and enact? Then our readings for Advent and Christmas open us to the fullness of who we human creatures are and what we can do. Christmas remakes worldly realism into holy realism. Herod perpetuates his violence, but the Christ Child grows up to restore, to heal, and to bring good news to the poor (Matthew 11:2-6). Holy realism sees that although life is brutal, tragic, and hard, there is born in the midst of the world one who will draw out the glorious possibilities of the world's trans-formation. Holy realism is the realism of Advent and Christmas.

A Different Kind of Christmas Card

Year A, Advent 2: Matthew 3:1-12, Advent 3: Isaiah 35:1-10,
Advent 4: Matthew 1:18-25, Christmas 1: Isaiah 63:7-9

What will you say in your Christmas greeting card this year? I am always touched by those who send a brief account of their activities. I am glad to catch up and reestablish connections with people I have not recently seen. And I am equally delighted by those who make their own cards, often featuring the block print of a single word or image—"Peace," "Joy," "Glory," a star, an angel, a stable.

Imagine, then, if you were to create your Christmas greetings for this year, only instead of drawing on your personal activities from the last twelve months, you based your card on one of the four passages listed above. What words or images leap out that you would want to include on your card or in your letter? I can imagine a series of Advent sermons based on this question. Instead of telling people what the card and letter would contain, each sermon would be an invitation to join you in creating this year's greetings.

Take a look at Matthew 3:1-12. What key word or phrase would your card feature—"repent" "prepare," "burn"? I am drawn to John the Baptist's phrase "bear fruit worthy of repentance" (3:8 NRSV). These are severe words, reminding us that our preparation for the coming of Christ calls us to moral accountability and to making our faith manifest in all we say and do.

If I were to work from Isaiah 35:1-10, I might choose "the burning sand shall become a pool" (v. 7), because the image suggests the pain and desperation that so many in this world feel, and the promise of its transformation.

Drawing upon Matthew 1:18-25, I might create a block print of an angel, and my Christmas letter would be filled with stories of how God keeps intervening in unexpected ways at the most inconvenient times. For the angel does not show up until *after* Joseph has "planned" and "resolved" (1:19-20 NRSV, ESV) his own course of action. Joseph embodies the higher righteousness for which Matthew's Gospel calls: he gives up his own devising to welcome God's direction.

Or after examining Isaiah 63, perhaps my block print greeting would be "Lament!" because verses 7-19 are a communal lament recording how sad it is that Israel turned from God. Without such a lament for the community and ourselves we will never know the full joy of God seeking us out through Christ.

These are initial ruminations to start your own. Let your sermon be a different kind of Christmas card that opens your congregation to the challenging greetings that the Spirit of the living God brings us this Advent and Christmas.

Security in an Unsafe Neighborhood

Year A, Advent 3: Isaiah 35:1-10, Christmas 1: Matthew 2:13-23

I am an early morning walker. When I travel, I often ask a hotel clerk about the best place to walk. The clerk will usually observe either, "This is a safe neighborhood," or "We suggest that you use our athletic center rather than walk the streets this early in the morning." I am always filled with sadness to think that anyone cannot step boldly into God's creation because the neighborhood is not safe. When we feel surrounded by threats, security becomes an obsession. We create a new artificial environment of government agencies, gated communities, household alarm systems, metal detectors, body scanners, private security firms, and services to protect us from identity theft.

How do you find security when the whole world has become an unsafe neighborhood?

The question echoes through our Advent readings as we encounter both safe and dangerous neighborhoods. Isaiah describes a vision of a transformed world in which "waters will spring up in the desert, and streams in the wilderness" and where there is no threat of violence: "No lion will be there, / and no predator will go up on it" (Isaiah 35:6b, 9a). Redemption is living in a safe neighborhood! But after reading Isaiah's vision of security during Advent, we encounter at Christmas the slaughter of the innocents:

> A voice was heard in Ramah,
> > weeping and much grieving,
> > > Rachel weeping for her children,
> > > > and she did not want to be comforted,
> > > > > because they were no more. (Matthew 2:18)

I wonder if some of those parents whose babies were slaughtered thought they lived in a safe neighborhood until Herod's soldiers crashed through the door.

There are two different responses to a world that is unsafe. One is to try to find an enclave of security for you and your family. Joseph does this with some success: he escapes with Mary and the Child to Egypt. But that strategy seldom holds up over time. Some thirty years after the flight into Egypt, Jesus would be crucified under Pontius Pilate. The second strategy is the only one that will make the world a safe neighborhood: to incarnate in our lives the love and grace of the one whose birth we eagerly await.

A Word to Clarify the Shadows and Tangles of Life

Year A, Christmas Day: John 1:1-14

I have a friend to whom I turn when I am going through a tough patch. I love talking with him not just because he listens well, but also because he has an extraordinary capacity to clarify the shadows and tangles of my life with the briefest of words. I am so grateful for the light of his speech. Others might pile word on top of word and not provide me with half as much clarity.

I reflect on what his gift implies about preaching. Surely one of the things we preachers hope is that our words, like my friend's, will clarify the shadows and tangles of the congregation's life. Preaching, however, is not one-on-one conversation, and the outpouring of each listener's heart does not precede sermons. What, then, could make preaching as effective for a congregation as my friend's wise counsel is for me?

The obvious thing is for the preacher to know the heart of the congregation, their struggles and their delights. But knowing these is not enough. My friend offers more than a patient ear. He also presents me a word from outside of myself that is related to but not entangled with my predicament. I believe this gift replicates the pattern of what God is doing in Christ. John calls Christ "the Word" and then makes the astounding claim,

> The Word became flesh
> and made his home among us.
> We have seen his glory. (John 1:14a)

Since the Word becomes flesh and since flesh means not just the physical body but our humanity in its entirety, it follows that the Word is thoroughly related to us. The Word knows the shadows and tangles of human life.

But the Word also offers something more than identification—something far vaster than our subjective identity. The Word offers "glory" and "grace and truth." The Word confirms our humanity through willingness to become one of us, but in the act of doing so opens us to greater realities. That is what my friend does in a less cosmic way, and that is what effective preaching does when the Word becomes flesh through the words of the preacher.

For More Than the Sake of Angels

Year A, Christmas 1: Hebrews 2:10-18

Angels have been pouring into my house the last few weeks. Gabriel has shown up many times, usually with magnificent feathered wings. In addition to Gabriel, the heavenly host has made several appearances, all their mouths opened in song. I welcome them into my home when I open the Christmas cards that come with the mail each day during the weeks of Advent. My wife and I put some of the angel-bearing cards on our buffet: a flock of angels to stand around the nativity set.

I think of my far-flung friends who sent these cards and who wrote their annual greetings, often enclosing a letter about their comings and goings during the last year. As I read their words and look at the angels they chose to accompany their annual letters, I recall that the word *angel* means "messenger," and thus it strikes me as utterly appropriate that their letters, the news about their lives, should be brought to me by an angel. I discover in many of the letters not only notable achievements and happy milestones, but also news of people who have lost their jobs and are in financial distress, individuals awaiting serious medical procedures, and people who have died or are now facing death.

I bear in my heart the vision of angels and the both joyful and sad messages they have brought to my home when I read this passage—a passage I have never before preached on during Advent and Christmas: "Therefore, since the children share in flesh and blood, he also shared the same things in the same way. He did this to destroy the one who holds the power over death. . . . Of course, he isn't trying to help angels, but rather he's helping Abraham's descendants" (Hebrews 2:14, 16). These verses put Gabriel and the heavenly hosts who are filling my home into proper perspective. Yes, the angels are indeed lovely, but their heavenly splendor must not distract me from the core of the gospel: Christ has come not for the sake of angels but for us human creatures, fragile and broken as we are.

God's Love by Human Love Was Blessed

Years A, B, and C, Epiphany: Matthew 2:1-12

Many years ago a group home for children and youth commissioned me to write a hymn that would give thanks for the ministry of caring for young people displaced from their families of origin. For inspiration I turned to Matthew 2:1-12, the visit of the Magi. Here is the second stanza of the hymn:

> In Joseph's arms, at Mary's breast,
> while Herod's violence spread,
> God's love by human love was blessed,
> protected, nurtured, fed.[1]

Although the commissioners were pleased with the hymn, another group that wanted to use the words decided to omit this single stanza because they opposed the idea that human love can bless God's love. Yet the psalmists often command us to bless God: "Let my whole being bless the LORD! / Let everything inside me / bless his holy name!" (Psalm 103:1). Surely Mary nursing the infant Jesus and Joseph fleeing with mother and child to Egypt reveal that human love can bless divine love. Without the blessing of these faithful and courageous human actions, the Christ Child would have died for lack of nourishment or protection from the cruel and violent world.

The possibility of human love blessing the divine love of Christ does not end with the biblical story. We have just come through a season in which we have sung and prayed, "Let every heart prepare him room," and, "Where meek souls will receive him, still the dear Christ enters in." If Christ is born again here and now, if the story of Christ's nativity replays itself in our lives and the life of the world, then we need to ask how we are being called to bless the newly born love of God. Where does the vulnerable love of the infant Christ need protection? How does that love need to be nurtured and fed? To ask these questions does not diminish the power of God; rather it reveals the nature of that power. It is the power of a love that blesses us and that trusts we will return the blessing, even as Mary and Joseph did.

Count Everyone In

Years A, B, and C, Epiphany: Isaiah 60:1-6, Matthew 2:1-12, Ephesians 3:1-12

As a child I played a game in which some of us held hands in a circle while others ran from the outside and tried to break in. There was often a fierce intensity in playing the game. Part of it was the bodily energy of children involved in active play. But the concentration of those running to break in and of those holding hands to keep them out arose from something more: an unarticulated awareness that the game was about life, about the most basic issues of community and self-identity. It was about who is in and who is out, about how much energy we expend to break the circles formed against us, and how hard we work to keep intact the circles that make us secure against others.

Who is in and who is out is a pattern that is replayed again and again not only in our individual lives but also in our religious communities. Isaiah's was a vision that reversed the experience of the exiles, who felt as if God had locked them out of the circle of acceptance and value when they had been hauled away from their homeland to Babylon. Now they were to return, and their home was to become a beacon to others: "Nations will come to your light / and kings to your dawning radiance" (Isaiah 60:3). The boundaries of bitterness left from the Exile were to break down not through the spontaneous generosity of the people but through a shining forth of God's light (v. 1).

We encounter this light again in Matthew in the star that stirs the quest of the Magi. What an intriguing story for Matthew to put early in his Gospel. Matthew, who often pictures the horror awaiting those failing to make it into the kingdom, here shows an attractive openness to the stranger. It is as if Matthew were telling his community not to form a circle against strangers—not to hold them out but to welcome them in.

Ephesians gives us yet another slant on this repeated pattern of breaking open the exclusive circle: "This plan is that Gentiles would be coheirs and parts of the same body, and that they would share with the Jews in the promises of God in Christ Jesus through the gospel" (Ephesians 3:6). Although Isaiah, Matthew, and the author of Ephesians were each addressing particular historical situations, the pattern of breaking the circle of religious exclusion is repeated in each passage. And it is a pattern that we seek to repeat in our own time. Just as we hope that each generation of children will grow up to open the circle and count everyone in,

12

so too we work for a church that makes plain the inclusivity of the gospel: in Jesus Christ, all "have bold and confident access to God through faith in him" (Ephesians 3:12).

Do No Harm

T he first rule of medicine, "Do no harm," is also a fine first rule for preachers. Isaiah describes the ideal servant of God as one who will not break "a bruised reed" nor snuff out "a dimly burning wick" (Isaiah 42:3 NRSV).

Any time we preach, there are bruised reeds listening: people who have been stepped on by the world, by cruelty, abuse, exploitation, and prejudice. They need a preacher who does not break them with angry words, but who helps them to keep growing, to keep reaching for the light.

In every congregation there are dimly burning wicks, people who have just a glimmer of faith, a tiny flame of hope, an aching, a yearning, a seeking in the soul that is all they can muster. They need a preacher who does not snuff out whatever dim light flickers within them, but feeds the sputtering flame.

The tenderness of Isaiah's ideal servant arises from the experience of exile, from being violently conquered and hauled away to Babylon. The experience of suffering awakened the prophet (or school of prophets writing in Isaiah's name) to the need for tenderness. In a similar manner, there are preachers who acknowledge that they became effective only after suffering themselves or after seeing so much suffering in others. Their pastoral work reveals to them how easy it is to snap a bruised reed in two, or to put out a dimly burning wick. But after passing through great pain themselves and after weeping with so many others who weep, their hearts begin to go out to their listeners. Now their sermons help the bruised reeds to stand a little taller and less bent, and the dimly burning wicks to burn with a brighter flame.

It is revealing to note that Jesus' proclamation of the good news is accompanied by acts of compassion as he cures "every disease and sickness among the people" (Matthew 4:23). I wonder how much Christ's continual contact with those who suffered shaped his voice as a preacher, how much his pastoral work kept his preaching from breaking bruised reeds and snuffing out dim wicks. Because Christ was a preacher who did no harm, he was also able to call people to the hard work of repentance (Matthew 4:17).

Acute Hearing Restored

Year A, Epiphany 2: Psalm 40:1-11

Sometimes when I have been swimming I get out of the pool and discover that one of my ears is filled with water and I can barely hear through it. A similar thing happens to both ears when I am in an airplane that descends swiftly and the pressurized cabin system is not working well. I get off the plane and explain to my host that my ears are "popping," making it difficult to hear. In the case of the water-plugged ear, I tilt my head to the side and shake it, and the ear clears, while after the sudden plane descent, I find chewing a wad of gum will often open up my ears. Until I finish shaking or chewing, it is as if my ears are buried.

I was reminded of this experience when I looked at the translation note to Psalm 40:6a in the NRSV. The passage reads, "Sacrifice and offering you do not desire, but you have given me an open ear." The translation note at the bottom of the page informs us that the Hebrew reads, "ears you have dug for me." I was so intrigued by the idea of God digging out our ears that I consulted a number of other translations. One reads,

> You did not seek offerings
> or ask for sacrifices;
> but you drilled ears
> for me to hear.[2]

Another translates the phrase "You opened ears for me," and then provides a footnote: "The phrase literally means, 'You dug open ears [or, to]' —that is, vouchsafed me a new acute power of listening to the divine truth."[3] Whether we choose "drilling" or "digging," it is clear that this is a strenuous process—much more so than opening our physical ears when they are plugged from swimming or descending swiftly in an airplane.

As we move through Epiphany, a season that celebrates God's word being revealed to the world, we might pray:

O God, whose word brought forth the heavens and the earth and whose word is made manifest in Christ, dig out our ears anew, clearing away everything that muffles the voice of our incarnate Savior. Amen.

A Prayer for Preachers

Year A, Epiphany 9: Matthew 7:21-29

Having taught preaching for the last thirty-plus years, I have learned that there is one thing homiletical methods alone can never teach—yet it is one of the most important qualities for every preacher to have. I am thinking of *integrity*—the sense of a soul so deeply grounded in the truth that there is in the preacher's whole way of being a coherence, clarity, and trustworthiness of character that command our attentive listening whenever the person proclaims the word of God.

The ancient rhetoricians knew the importance of integrity, and noted how much the persuasiveness of an argument depended upon the character of the speaker. Matthew appears to share this conviction, ending the Sermon on the Mount with an observation about the compelling quality of Christ's teaching: "Now when Jesus had finished saying these things, the crowds were astounded at his teaching, for he taught them as one having authority, and not as their scribes" (Matthew 7:28-29 NRSV). As the official experts in the Law, the scribes supposedly had the skill and position to win a hearing for what they taught. Yet their authority paled when compared to the effect of Jesus' teaching upon the crowd. Even after allowing for Matthew's polemical agendas, I believe we are left with a witness to the character of Jesus: there was about his person an incorruptible integrity that gave his words a power greater than that of the established authorities. People sensed that Jesus' speech was sustained by the core of who he was. They responded to what he said because they knew it was backed up by the substance of his character. When Jesus called Matthew to follow him, the tax collector "got up and followed him" (Matthew 9:9). Afterwards, when Jesus took heat from the authorities for associating with such disreputable people, he did not cave in, but stuck by his word (Matthew 9:10-12).

The formation of our character, then, is a homiletical discipline every bit as crucial to our preaching as the exposition of Scripture and the search for vivid ways to communicate with the congregation. How well does my life incarnate what I proclaim? That is a prayer for preachers to offer God week by week as they prepare their sermons.

Spirituality: No Genie in a Bottle

Year A, Transfiguration (Sunday before Ash Wednesday): Exodus 24:12-18, Lent 1: Matthew 4:1-11

Spirituality is in and *religion* is out. At least that is what is reported about large numbers of Americans in the popular press and in works on the sociology of religion. Bookstores confirm this shift in popular idiom. Instead of *religion* or *theology*, I find sections of shelves marked *spirituality*.

There are multiple ways to view this cultural trend, but for now I want to pursue just one: the light that the Scriptures cast upon spiritual discipline, a theme that emerges in at least two texts as we move into Lent, Exodus 24:12-18 (Moses receiving the Law) and Matthew 4:1-11 (the temptations of Jesus in the wilderness).

When I read the blurbs on popular books about contemporary "spirituality," one of the things that strikes me is how often these books present spiritual disciplines as a recipe for cooking up a particular result: there are ten ways to inner peace, seven principles to becoming centered. Spirituality is reduced to method, allowing us to create and control spiritual experience. It is a concept that fits comfortably with our technological age in which we build worlds that we command.

The Bible offers a different kind of spirituality. For example, Moses' encounter with the divine and Jesus' temptations both take place in the context of "forty days and forty nights." This is a formulaic phrase suggesting a time of intentional spiritual discipline, but the results are different for each man. "Forty days and forty nights" brings the Torah to Moses and the tempter to Jesus. Holding the two passages next to each other, we learn that God is not ours to control, that spiritual discipline does not guarantee a given result. Authentic spirituality can open us to the most troubling elements of reality as well as to God.

Biblical spirituality is a corrective to the distortions of a culture that always wants to be in control. We do not conjure up the Spirit like a genie from a bottle. Instead our spiritual discipline opens us to the full range of forces that shape the core of our being. Biblical spirituality keeps us open to possibilities we cannot predict or command.

Suckers for the Talking Snake

Year A, Lent 1: Genesis 2:15-17; 3:1-7

WWould the story in the garden of Eden have ended differently if some preacher had delivered a homily to Adam and Eve?

"Count your blessings, Adam and Eve. You have each other's companionship, beautiful surroundings, ample streams, gold, bdellium, onyx stone, cattle, birds of the air, animals of the field, and an astounding variety of fruit trees. Except for a particular fruit that you are not to eat, you have free rein of the place. What more could you ask? You live in paradise. Count your blessings.

"Uh oh, here comes the snake. Whatever you do, Adam and Eve, do not listen to that sly creature. When the snake talks, turn away and count your blessings until the snake gives up. Remember the list I gave you. You are blessed with each other's companionship, beautiful surroundings, ample streams, gold, bdellium, onyx stone, cattle, birds of the air, animals of the field, and an astounding variety of fruit trees."

That homily would not have made one bit of difference. Already blessed extravagantly, Adam and Eve—you and I—always want more. We are suckers for the talking snake. There is something in us constantly reaching beyond the extravagant blessings that are already ours. Counting the material wealth of our lives only makes us more susceptible to the snake. What we have makes us want more.

The Beatitudes (Matthew 5:1-12) are the antidote to the snake's palaver. Instead of the promise of powers lying beyond our finitude—"You will see clearly and you will be like God" (Genesis 3:4)—Christ directs us to consider those who are already blessed by their poverty of spirit, by their grief, and by their hunger for what is good. The snake directs us to cast a longing glance beyond paradise. But Christ roots our blessings in the very things that the world considers signs of weakness and failure: meekness, mourning, peacemaking, and persecution.

When we count our tears to be a blessing, we will no longer be suckers for the talking snake. It is easier for the wily creature to succeed in an environment that is rich and luscious than in the heart that hungers for righteousness and comfort.

Anything Getting Through?

Year A, Lent 4: Psalm 23

As a small child I used to visit my mother's hometown in rural South Carolina every summer. I remember the church services vividly, the robust singing of hymns and the fans that were in the pew racks: each was a wide piece of cardboard stapled to a tongue depressor. This was before the church had air conditioning, and since I was in a dress shirt with a suit and tie, and since the humidity was often 100 percent and the temperature nearly 100 degrees, I was very appreciative of those fans. On one side of the fan was an advertisement, sometimes for a funeral parlor, sometimes for a car dealership. On the other side of every fan was the Twenty-third Psalm in the King James Version with a picture of Jesus in a rich purple robe, carrying a staff and a little lamb.

I would wave the fan energetically until I grew tired. Then I would stop and study the picture of the Good Shepherd. I did not need to read the psalm because my mother had recited it so many times that I already knew it by heart. I spent most of my non-fanning time just staring at Jesus and the lamb in his arms and silently reciting the psalm to myself while the preacher preached on.

Some people might brush this off as a sentimental recollection. But in remembering it, I appreciate anew how formative such experiences can be to the life of faith. Some fifty years later my mother was dying and I was at her bedside. People often say at such times that they have no words to speak. But my mother and I had the words we needed, words that extended all the way back into my childhood when I was dependent upon her and not she upon me. "The LORD is my shepherd; I shall not want. . . . Yea, though I walk through the valley of the shadow of death, I will fear no evil: for thou art with me; thy rod and thy staff they comfort me" (Psalm 23:1, 4 KJV).

Remember this story the next time you see a child in church and wonder if anything is getting through.

Starting Assumptions

Year A, Lent 3: John 4:5-42, Lent 5: Ezekiel 37:1-14,
Easter Day, John 20:1-18,
Years A, B, and C, Palm/Passion Sunday: Philippians 2:5-11

good

W hen two people are locked into an argument, the solution seldom lies in discovering whose reasoning is faulty or sound.
Each one's reasoning may be faultless. The difficulty is not in
the chain of thought but the different starting assumptions.

What is true of arguments between people is also true of the way we
respond to life. Perhaps our starting assumptions include the following:

- Death is the irrevocable end of individuals and institutions.
- We cannot break through centuries of racial and sexual
  stereotyping.
- Humility always loses to power.

As church people, we may deny these are our starting assumptions. But
when we consider how we and our congregations live, it often appears
that these are in fact the assumptions that shape our actions in the world.

Many of our readings from Lent to Palm Sunday to Easter turn our
starting assumptions upside down. The dead bones of Israel are re-knit
(Ezekiel 37:1-14). A gracious rabbi breaks through the barrier between
men and women, between Jews and Samaritans (John 4:5-42). Christ is
raised (John 20:1-18). The humble one who "did not consider being
equal / with God something to exploit" is honored at every level of reality, "in heaven, on earth, / and under the earth" (Philippians 2:5, 11).

Many of these passages contain a dramatic turning point in which the
old starting assumption asserts itself and then crumbles before the gracious action of God. The Samaritan woman's first response to Jesus is
astonishment based on ancient prejudices, "Why do you, a Jewish man,
ask for something to drink from me, a Samaritan woman?" (John 4:9).
Mary at the tomb assumes the risen Christ is the gardener (John 20:15).
Paul, before quoting the hymn about Christ's self-emptying character,
first reminds the Philippians not to act on the basis of the world's starting
assumptions: "Don't do anything for selfish purposes" (Philippians 2:3).

All these texts transform our starting assumptions. Now we trust that:

- Death opens individuals and institutions to new life.
- It *is* possible to break through centuries of racial and sexual stereotyping.
- Humility transfigures power.

When these become our starting assumptions, we see openings for new life that our finest reasoning, based on our old assumptions, would never have dreamed possible.

Is It Possible to Change the World?

Years A, B, and C, Palm/Passion Sunday: Philippians 2:5-11

Is it possible to change the world? Day by day, hour by hour on my iPad, on the radio, and on television the news reports are of unceasing terror and violence. There may be new names and new places, but the story line is the same: hate begets hate, terror begets terror, violence begets violence. Even if we are not the immediate victims, the worst of human nature takes a toll on our spirits. We begin to withdraw from the world, to hoard our energies and expend them only upon ourselves and upon those we love.

Is it possible to change the world? *No* is the answer, if in fact the only force at work in the world is the ingrained pattern of protecting our power at all costs and retaliating for every offense against us. Then I would conclude that it is not possible to change the world.

But what if there are other forces that have been set free in the world, other currents that are rising from the deep, dear core of things? The Apostle Paul believes that Christ has initiated ways of using power that can reshape the world:

> Adopt the attitude that was in Christ Jesus:
> Though he was in the form of God,
> he did not consider being equal
>   with God as something to exploit.
> But he emptied himself
> by taking the form of a slave. (Philippians 2:5-7a)

Paul says in effect: align yourself with the very way of perceiving, knowing, being, and acting (mind) that was in Christ. It astounds me that Paul could make such a bold claim from prison after all the violence he had seen and experienced firsthand. Yet here he is confidently proclaiming the possibility of radical change—change that the world would have us doubt is possible. If we have the same mind that was in Christ, we will be changed, and it *will* be possible to change the world.

Blood and Water and Hope

Years A, B, and C, Good Friday: John 18:1–19:42

One of the soldiers pierced his side with a spear, and immediately blood and water came out" (John 19:34). What emotion must have been released when these words were read in John's community! There they were: a group of people who had lost fellow believers to the bloody Roman persecution, a group of people who had met at the Lord's table and tasted the blood of salvation.

Blood. Primal and elemental. Blood is life. Spilled blood is death. If you have ever witnessed a severe accident or a shooting or been in the front lines of battle, then you have seen blood, and you have known the terror of it: the vital fluid splattered and darkening the ground, the sidewalk, the street. O God, the fear of it! The way the breath is taken away, not just by the sight but by all that it signifies: the terror, the violence, the passion in the human heart that explodes and destroys other human beings.

How do we face such terror? How do we have hope that we will ever find the grace to overcome the forces that drive us to spill one another's blood? Surely these questions have been alive ever since Abel's blood was heard crying, crying from the ground, and surely these questions were still alive in John's community.

To hear that blood and water flowed from Jesus' pierced side gave them the answer: the one through whom all things were made has known the terror of our bloody ways. Blood has flowed from his side, a human carcass pierced open by a spear. Yet along with his blood flowed water, the sign of baptism, the sign of entrance into a community of peace.

Blood and water. Communion and baptism. When John's community heard about the blood and water flowing from Christ's side, they were probably filled with the memory of their baptisms and with all the times they had drunk of the cup of salvation. Then they realized with renewed power the meaning of these sacraments: God is with us, with us in our terror, in our blood-bathed world, with us to redeem us from this madness.

The water marks us as Christ's forever. It reminds us that our most essential identity is not with the cruel and hateful fury of this world, but with the one who is here among us to give us the grace and strength to transform this world.

Remember the water. Remember the blood. See them flowing from Jesus' side as vividly as John's community did, and find in that vision not simply terror and revulsion at how the world responds to love, but find there the identification of the divine with us in order that we will courageously stop the spilling of blood and be the community God intends.

Unseasonable Resurrection

Years A, B, and C, Easter Day: John 20:1-18

Some years Easter comes early enough that in the northern regions of the United States we may awaken to a late snowfall. Popular piety hopes for a flowering Easter and a white Christmas. The seasonal associations are not necessarily biblical, but they are very strong in the habits of our thought, including our homiletical thought. What could be more natural than for preachers to point to the wonder of new shoots sprouting and new blooms, springing to life as an emblem of resurrection?

Perhaps an early Easter, especially if there is a chill in the air or snow on the ground, can be an opportunity for framing resurrection with deeper understandings than an allusion to the blossoming flowers. Instead of associating Easter with the natural order of things, we can associate the resurrection of Christ with the radical disruption of finitude, with the resilience of the divine vitalities, with the intrusion of grace when we have reduced existence to the bounds of human limitation, with the unexpected opening of new possibilities when we have concluded that we are trapped in a morass of corruption and violence, with the renewal of life when we think death has triumphed, with the persistence of love when we believe hate has wiped it out, with the restoration of our visionary powers when we think we have lost the power to dream great dreams, and with the stranger who turns out to be not the gardener but the very one whom the world has crucified.

Our world is desperate to hear of the unseasonable resurrection of Christ because we have entered a long, fierce season of human brutality and environmental degradation. Preaching the resurrection can restore our people's hope and strength to engage the world with God's transforming life. For we have more than the memory of a dead teacher's wisdom. We have his empowering presence in our lives. Let this be the blessing of Easter whether we celebrate it in winter or spring: the realization of possibilities that our despairing hearts would never have seen except for the resurrection of Christ.

Delayed Recognition

Years A, B, and C, Easter Day: John 20:1-18, Easter 2: John 20:19-31

There is a repeated detail in three of the resurrection appearances of Christ that has momentous implications for the life of faith. Christ is not recognized at first by Mary in the garden, nor by the disciples gathered behind locked doors, nor by the party of followers that goes fishing. Mary initially supposes Christ to be a gardener and only identifies him when he calls her by name (John 20:16). The disciples cowering inside the locked room do not begin to rejoice at seeing their Lord until after he says, "Peace be with you," and shows them his hands and side (John 20:19-20). The fishing party obeys the instructions to cast the net on the other side of the boat without any attention to who is instructing them until after they catch so many fish they are unable to haul in the load (John 21:4-7). In every case the recognition of the risen Christ is delayed. It is not enough for Christ to appear. He has to call Mary by name; he has to speak and demonstrate his presence to the disciples.

This repeated detail in John's resurrection stories suggests that his community was consistently slow to recognize the risen Christ. Perhaps John is using this pattern to sharpen the community's awareness, to make them more persistent in considering where and when the risen Christ is appearing to them in their lives here and now. For by the time John writes his gospel there has been enough persecution and disappointment that the congregation may be replicating the same patterns of failing to recognize

Christ that we see in the resurrection stories handed down from the first generations of believers.

We often repeat that pattern ourselves. I recall asking a group of several hundred people at a conference to break into small groups and share when and where they had encountered the risen Christ. Many of them reported stories of delayed recognition, an awareness that came upon them only after the experience. I can imagine a series of sermons during Eastertide on the delayed recognition of the risen Christ. The sermons would help us look anew at the surprising and frequently unobserved presence of Christ in our daily life.

Off the Record

Years A, B, and C, Easter 2: John 20:19-31

At the conclusion of the story about doubting Thomas, John acknowledges, "Then Jesus did many other miraculous signs in his disciples' presence, signs that aren't recorded in this scroll" (John 20:30). I am curious about those other signs. What were they? And why is John so candid about admitting he left them off the record? Perhaps, since a community of believers helped John write his Gospel, he felt obligated to confess that he did not use everything that people reported to him. This way, if someone's favorite story were left out, the person might at least be placated by John's honesty, while continuing to tell the story to children and grandchildren and other members of the community.

All of this makes for a plausible explanation. But the impact of the verse is greater than a simple apology to those whose contribution did not make the evangelist's sermon! John's little disclaimer makes an important theological statement: namely, that the resurrection of Christ is a reality greater than what is recorded in print, even the print of the Bible. The Risen One shows up in far more than the stories that have been recorded in print. Christ does "many other signs *in the presence* of his disciples."

John's aside about what he has not written down turns out to be a theological observation of major importance. It reminds us not to limit our understanding of the risen Savior to the pages of the Bible but to look for Christ's signs *in the presence of his disciples*. I can imagine a series of sermons that uses John's acknowledgment about the limits of his witness as a justification for exploring many different places in history and in your church's life where the risen Christ has appeared.

After Easter there is usually a dramatic decrease in attendance at services, but those attendees who continue to celebrate the season of Easter often know from their faithful church participation that Christ does indeed perform signs "in his disciples' presence." It is always self-defeating to attack the people who are not there, and I never encourage such a strategy for preachers. But it would be heartening for those who are there to use the Sundays of Eastertide to celebrate Christ's "signs in his disciples' presence." Preach about the good things that have happened through church fellowship: the support for someone who lost a job, the strength a group has received to carry on a new mission, a prayer that brought comfort or healing. Hold before your people what is "not written in this book" but what is wonderfully apparent in the church's corporate life at its best: Christ is doing "many other miraculous signs in his disciples' presence."

How Do We Recognize the Risen Christ?

Year A, Easter 3: Luke 24:13-35, Easter 4: John 10:1-10

If you have ever had to pick up a stranger at an airport or train station, you know how frustrating a general description is: "Medium height and build, wearing jeans and a jacket." You appreciate knowing something more definitive: "I'll have on a red plaid scarf and a gray tweed overcoat." If we are going to follow Christ throughout our lives, then we need some way of answering the question, how do we recognize the risen Christ? Judging from many biblical passages, that question was a concern to the early church. In several passages we read about encounters and metaphors that help us identify how Christ is present in our lives.

The recognition of Christ is sometimes slow in coming. Consider the two disciples on the road to Emmaus. They travel several miles listening to Christ without recognizing their friend. But when they break bread together, then they recall, "Weren't our hearts on fire when he spoke to us along the road and when he explained the scriptures for us?" (Luke 24:32). Have you ever had a profound conversation with someone about suffering, death, and meaning, a conversation that awakened intensities of thought and feeling that put your whole life in a richer, deeper, wiser perspective? Perhaps the risen Christ was moving through that person toward you.

Have you ever found yourself attending to someone whose voice conveyed compassion, awaking in you a sense of security, serenity, and gratitude for that person's trustworthy care of you or of someone you love (John 10:4)? Perhaps the risen Christ was moving through that person toward you.

Have you ever found a community that revealed to you an abundance of life (John 10:10), a way of being and doing that was overflowing with grace and delight? Perhaps the risen Christ was moving through them toward you.

How do we recognize Christ? We listen to what is awakened in our hearts by our deepest conversations. We attend to the voices of compassion. We participate in a community of abundant life. Then we know that Christ is risen indeed. Alleluia, Alleluia!

Far Better Than a Visitation of Angels

Year A, Easter 3: Luke 24:13-35, Easter 5: John 14:1-14

I remember walking out of a worship service one day in which the final hymn was "Spirit of God, Descend upon My Heart." The second stanza opens,

> I ask no dream, no prophet ecstasies,
> No sudden rending of the veil of clay,
> No angel visitant, no opening skies.

One of my friends said to me, "I sang it, but I don't know if I mean it. I would welcome a prophet's ecstasy, a rending of the veil, an angel, an opening of the skies. I would settle for any of them!"

My friend's voice comes back to me over the years as I turn to the Gospel of John and find Philip insisting, "Lord, show us the Father; that will be enough for us" (John 14:8). The heart that scrambles desperately for a direct view of the divine is apt to miss what is right at hand. Jesus responds to Philip, "Don't you know me, Philip, even after I have been with you all this time? Whoever has seen me has seen the Father" (John 14:9). When the disciples felt most bereft, most abandoned by God, they suddenly discovered the Holy One was with them.

There is no story that more dramatically presents being surprised by Christ in our midst than the road to Emmaus. The two disciples who are trudging home are devastated. They tell the stranger who walks beside them: "We had hoped he was the one who would redeem Israel" (Luke 24:21). Then they share bread with the stranger, and their eyes are opened and they recognize Christ.

My friend, who had questioned the hymn because he craved assurance, sat down with me for coffee after the service. We had a rich conversation about the deepest spiritual hungers of our lives. When we got up, we both had a sense that something holy had happened between us. The heavens had not opened and there had been no rending of the veil of clay, but we were deeply satisfied. We had experienced something far better than a visitation of angels. We had left the table with "our hearts on fire" (Luke 24:32).

Never Out of Breath

Year A, Easter 6: John 14:15-21, Easter 7: Acts 2:6-14,
Pentecost: John 20:19-23, Trinity Sunday: Genesis 1:1–2:4a

I will never forget the first time I climbed a fourteen-thousand-foot peak. I set out early at a steady pace. But hours later, after I had passed the timberline at eleven thousand feet, I began stopping every ten or twelve steps to gasp the thinning air. I eventually realized that if I pressed on to the summit, the last few miles of my return trip would be by night. I turned around, defeated and winded.

I wonder if God realized how much wind it would take to keep the world going. In the beginning God sends a wind to sweep over the face of the waters (Genesis 1:2). The author of the opening creation story, though writing poetically, knew about the physics of force and energy, and to stir a wind that can separate the waters of the deep takes a massive amount of both. On the seventh day, "God rested from all the work of creation" (Genesis 2:3).

God rests, but God is never out of breath. Are we, like the community of John, exhausted by the terrors of the world and uncertain about how to find our way amidst confusion and conflict? God sends the "Spirit of Truth" to abide in us (John 14:17). Do we feel we have forgiven all we can forgive? Christ breathes the Holy Spirit upon us to renew our capacity to be merciful and gracious (John 20:19-23). Are we wondering where the church will find the strength to fulfill its calling? Christ assures us we will receive power when the Spirit comes upon us (Acts 1:8).

During trying times when people's energies often flag, we need to preach that God, who breathed upon the deep, keeps breathing the Spirit into us to help us find the truth, forgive one another, and carry on Christ's mission. I had to abandon my climb because I was too winded, but our Creator is never defeated for lack of breath. God continues to breathe upon us the Spirit of truth, the Spirit of grace, the Spirit of renewed energy for the mission of Christ.

What You Absolutely Must Do Today

Year A, Easter 7: John 17:1-11, Pentecost: John 7:37-39,
Trinity Sunday: Genesis 1–2:4a

What is on your list of things to do today? What is it that you cannot put off any longer?

Lists, whether we write them or store them in our memory, are one of the ways we attempt to keep the chaos monster at bay. Perhaps you remember the chaos monster from your introductory course in the Old Testament. The monster had a name in Babylonian mythology: Tiamat. A nasty brute was Tiamat. The monster makes a more subtle appearance in Genesis 1:2, defanged and demythologized as *tehom* (the deep).

In my experience the chaos monster appears again and again and is no respecter of lists. The unexpected phone call, the e-mail bearing tragic news, the reports of another bombing, another killing: the chaos monster is everywhere, from the details of daily life to the disasters and conflicts that plague the planet.

Although lists are a poor defense against the chaos monster, there is a way of ordering things that can give us strength to endure and can heal the ravages of the beast. The Gospels give witness to what should be at the top of every list: "Desire first and foremost God's kingdom and God's righteousness" (Matthew 6:33), and "This is eternal life: to know you, the only true God, and Jesus Christ whom you sent" (John 17:3). Seeking and

---

knowing God does not automatically defeat the chaos monster, but it opens us to the irrepressible resilience of the divine vitalities, to those "rivers of living water" (John 7:38) that flow as a gift of the Spirit through the hearts of the faithful.

Try this the next time you are listing what you absolutely must get done today. Put at the top of the list: *Seek the reign of God. Know God and Christ.* Let these realities frame all the other pressing things you have to do, and you may then discover, as you work your way through your list, that you are moving deeper and deeper into the truth of God, and that eternal life is not an unending progression of time, but a dimension of being that awakens gratitude and wonder.

Home for Pentecost

Years A, B, and C, Pentecost: Acts 2:1-21

One of the simplest ways to expand the preaching possibilities of an overworked lection is to do a word study. For example, Acts 2:1 begins the celebrated account of the coming of the Holy Spirit to the church: "When Pentecost Day arrived . . ." The word *Pentecost* occurs only one more time in all of Acts, but Luke, whom tradition posits as the author, uses the term in a way that is highly suggestive for sermons: "Paul had decided to sail past Ephesus so that he wouldn't need to spend too much time in the province of Asia. *He was hurrying to reach Jerusalem, if possible, by Pentecost Day*" (Acts 20:16, emphasis added). Home for Pentecost!

One way to interpret the passage is that Paul still kept some of the observances of his upbringing, since Pentecost was originally a Jewish holy day. But another possibility, especially when we consider the story line of Acts, is that the verse is telling us about the importance of periodically returning to the revelatory experience of the Spirit that has set loose the dynamic activity of the church. Think of all that has happened in the book of Acts between chapters 2 and 20: Peter and John's questioning before the authorities, persecutions at the hands of opponents, Paul's conversion, Peter's vision of all things made clean, the death of James, the establishment of many new congregations, the Jerusalem council on Jewish-Gentile relationships, the baptism of Lydia and her household, Paul's sermon in Athens, the riot in Ephesus. And all of this is only a partial list of the tumultuous, passionate gathering of mission and witness to Christ in the early church.

Perhaps Luke was feeling how the story had mushroomed into a sprawling epic in which the reader might forget that the church's growth was more than the work of a few headstrong individuals. It was—for Luke—the work of the Spirit, and the description of Paul returning to Jerusalem for Pentecost portrays an apostle who never forgot that the source and sustainer of his ministry was the Spirit that had come to the church as fire and wind.

Paul's eagerness to be in "Jerusalem, if possible, by Pentecost Day," is a reminder to us busy church people that there is a need to get home for Pentecost, to return to the source who called and mobilized our ministries in the first place. There is a danger in this: we may try to re-create an original spiritual experience that belongs now to the past. But there is also a hope: that we will renew our openness to the uncontrolled and ineffable reality that guides all authentic ministry.

Love for a Miniscule Mote

Years A, B, and C, Trinity Sunday: Psalm 8

I have in my personal library a stunning book of photographs of stars, galaxies, interstellar dust, nebulae, and other astronomical phenomena.[4] I find myself utterly mesmerized by these images that were taken from various observatories around the world as well as by the Hubble telescope that orbits above our planet. I look and look and look at these images, my amazement and wonder only heightened by the written descriptions that accompany them: "Some of the images reproduced here depict vistas whose photons started their long journey toward us well before *Homo sapiens* arose on this miniscule mote of oxygenated, irrigated earth."[5] Some of the stars "have burned steadily since they first ignited a few million years after the Big Bang, 13.7 billion years ago."[6] The author, without espousing a religious conviction, still finds himself driven to language that borders on the numinous: "It's a miracle, of course,"[7] and it "allows for a consideration of Mystery."[8] He condenses the effect of contemplating these wonders to a pungent line from the great English poet

William Blake (1757–1827): "Eternity is in love with the productions of time."

I place the book aside and start reading one of the psalms assigned by the lectionary:

> When I look up at your skies,
> at what your fingers made—
> the moon and the stars
> that you set firmly in place—
>   what are human beings
>   that you think about them,
>   what are human beings
>   that you pay attention to them? (Psalm 8:3-4)

I return to the book of galaxies and interstellar dust, and I read again about "this miniscule mote of oxygenated, irrigated earth." Amidst a universe "about 93 billion light-years wide" God loves "this miniscule mote," and, even more astonishing, loves all who dwell on it. I find myself praying:

> *You in whom we live and move and have our being, may our science make us wise, opening us to the wonder that reminds us how infinitely small yet eternally loved we are in this universe beyond mortal comprehension.*

I am not sure I have a sermon yet, but I have a heart flooded with gratitude and astonishment, and that is a splendid state of soul for any preacher.

Start at the End

Ordinary Time and Preaching about Final Things

I have a mental trick that I use whenever I face something painful that is impossible to avoid, such as a medical operation or a personal confrontation. I start at the end. I imagine what it will be like after it is all over, after I am healed or after the air has been cleared. The vision at the end redefines the current difficulty, the struggle, and the fear. Of course, not all things come out exactly as I imagine, and sometimes, sadly, the situation becomes more serious. But in many cases, it is that vision of a better future coming toward me that makes it possible to slog through the present, to bear the pain, to take on the demons, to find the strength for a struggle that seems overwhelming.

My little mental strategy is but a small human variation on the much larger theological theme that occupies many of the biblical writers, from prophets like Isaiah, who envisioned God doing a new thing, to apocalyptic seers like John, who fed their powers of spiritual survival with fantastic visions of a world where God's city comes to earth and the divine dwells with humanity. Sometimes these biblical visions move toward bloody vengeance, and they present a violent God who is repugnant to us, especially when we think of the terrors that have resulted from people considering themselves the agents of heaven's vengeance.

Nevertheless, the visionary impulse and the eschatological hope of biblical writers present us with an important principle: the inadequacy of a religious perspective that is bound only to the past and present. When there is no hope, no imagining, no dreaming of the better world that we in partnership with God may create, then our powers to endure and to press onward atrophy.

The spirituals of African Americans give witness to the continuation of the biblical pattern of eschatological hope. The work of black theologians in recent decades has helped us see that these songs functioned not only to provide the promise of a life beyond this life, but were often also the accompaniment to escape and rebellion.

As we preach through Ordinary Time, we ought to join the tradition of biblical seers and black singers by developing a homiletical eschatology. Our view of the future will not fill every sermon, but it will enlighten our process of homiletical creativity by getting us to imagine the world we would like our preaching to foster. What would congregational life look like if the church worked through the conflicts that have it in knots? What vision do we have for our community that would come to be if our words moved people to mission? What high, holy vision do you want your preaching to feed and build—not just for this or that particular Sunday, but for your preaching over time? I am well acquainted with the negative voices that arise in us preachers: "Be realistic." "Preaching cannot make that big a difference." "It is enough to be ready for next Sunday." These are not the voices of a vital homiletic. They reduce preaching to nothing more than a weekly chore. And the consequences are devastating: No vision, no fire. No dream, no new world. No imagining, no doing.

As you move into Ordinary Time, begin with the best aspirations of your heart for the world your words may help to birth. Preach eschatologically: start at the end to find renewed energy for the beginning.

The Grace of Law

Year A, Proper 4: Deuteronomy 11:18-21, 26-28 (alternate first reading)

Preachers often present *law* and *grace* as opposites: the law does not save us. Grace does. Although there is profound truth in this distinction that is well worth exploring in many a sermon, there is also a counter-truth. Instead of law being the opposite of grace, law can also be a means of grace. I am indebted here to Werner Lemke, a former professor of Old Testament interpretation, with whom I studied. I recall distinctly a powerful lecture that he gave explaining that law was for the devout Jew a way of grace.

To understand the grace of law, it is helpful to compare the Lord, who reveals clearly what is expected of us mortals, with other ancient deities whose ways were totally and utterly obscured from human knowledge. For example, here are excerpts from a Sumero-Akadian prayer to every god:

> May the fury of my lord's heart be quieted toward me.
> May the god who is not known be quieted toward me;
> May the goddess who is not known be quieted toward me.
> May the god whom I know or do not know be quieted toward me;
> May the goddess whom I know or do not know be quieted toward me,
>
> . . . .
>
> The transgression which I have committed, indeed I do not know;
> The sin which I have done, indeed I do not know.
> The forbidden thing which I have eaten, indeed I do not know;
> The prohibited (place) on which I have set foot, indeed I do not know.[9]

There is a desperation about this prayer that is heart wrenching. The supplicant is not only in dire straits but has no way of knowing what he or she has done wrong because it has not been in any way revealed.

Contrast this desperation with the book of Deuteronomy in which God clearly names what is expected: "Pay attention! I am setting blessing and curse before you right now" (Deuteronomy 11:26a). The Lord reveals what the Lord desires. The grace of law is this: God makes clear what is expected of us.

When the Bad Guys Turn Out Good

Year A, Proper 5: Matthew 9:9-13, 18-26

Most movies have their good guys and bad guys. It is clear who is good and who is bad, and one of the ways a film holds our attention is by awakening our hope that the good guys will win and the bad guys will get their well-deserved comeuppance. Hollywood generally gives us our wish, allowing us to have in cinematic fantasy what we seldom experience in life.

Imagine Matthew presenting his Gospel as a possible film script to some Hollywood producers. They read it through and decide to phone him. "Very interesting script here, Matt. Very clear who the real good guy is: Jesus. Healing and all. Very nice. Very good. That will play well. But after him, we've got some real problems. And some of the biggest of those problems are with what Jesus does as the good guy. He does not lay a trap for the bad guys. He does not blow them up. He says: 'I have come to call not the good guys but the bad guys' (see Matthew 9:13). Now, that is not going to play well. Jesus is eating with them. Hanging out with them. He should not do that. He should be plotting how to blow them up, shoot them down, end the miserable scoundrels' lives!"

"But that's not what Jesus does," Matthew responds. "Jesus has no intention of shooting them. He wants to rescue the bad guys from their badness."

"Get real, Matt. Who is going to buy a ticket to see a movie where the bad guys end up coming out on top?"

"That is not exactly what happens. It's not that the bad guys come out on top. It's that they become friends with the one truly good guy. His goodness transforms their badness, takes it away, and reshapes them into something that they could have been all along but never were before he befriended them."

"Matt, can we negotiate a more marketable story?"

"No, I will not compromise the gospel. What I have written will never satisfy your plot lines. But let me suggest something else: try out in your own life what I have written in my script."

Press Star Nine to Return to the Menu

Year A, Proper 6: Romans 5:1-8

I phone to get information and hear a recorded voice: "Please listen carefully to the menu because our options have recently changed." I listen to the whole menu. Not one option suggests the information I need. A voice tells me: "Press star nine to return to the menu." I do and take a guess at which option might possibly lead to the information I seek. No luck. I hit star nine again and try another option. No luck. I continue repeating the process. At long last I hit the right number and finally make contact with a person who in a matter of seconds tells me what I phoned to find out in the first place.

I fear that our preaching may sometimes make the grace of God seem as inaccessible as the options offered by voice mail or an overly complex website. How easy it is to get lost in some convoluted exegetical detail or to present our thoughts so that a listener wonders which one of the many paths we have laid out in a sermon leads to God.

The Apostle Paul makes a statement that is worth remembering whenever our preaching becomes as labored as a phone menu: "We have peace with God through our Lord Jesus Christ. We have access by faith into this grace in which we stand" (Romans 5:1b–2a). Notice how the entire statement is in the indicative: not we *should* find peace with God, but "we *have* peace with God." Not we *must* gain access to grace, but "we *have* access by faith into this grace in which we stand." The gospel does not depend on our hitting some right combination of theological buttons. God has already acted through Christ to grant us the grace and peace that we need. When this reality is fixed in the preacher's heart and mind, then there is a refreshing clarity of vision, a bracing confidence to declare what God generously provides.

What would happen to our preaching if all our sermons sprang from this gracious conviction? There would be no need to press star nine and start through the menu all over again!

Who Calls the Tune?

Year A, Proper 9: Matthew 11:16-19, 25-30, Proper 12: Romans 8:26-39

The place of music in Christian worship was a hotly debated topic during the first centuries of the church's existence. Because music was a prominent feature in pagan ceremonies, church leaders feared its use in worship would blur the distinctive identity of the Christian community. The matter was resolved for the early church when Christian theologians, drawing on the work of Pythagoras, concluded that music offered as prayer brought people into harmony with the music of the spheres, the music of heaven.

The early church's debate about music came to mind as I read Jesus' words: "[This generation] is like a child sitting in the marketplaces calling out to others, 'We played the flute for you, and you didn't dance. We sang a funeral song and you didn't mourn'" (Matthew 11:16-17). Instead of seeking to be in harmony with the music of heaven (Jesus), the world wants Jesus to dance to its song.

Who calls the tune in our lives? The metaphor is implicitly present in Paul's description of how the Spirit "intercedes" with its own kind of music, with "sighs too deep for words" that are tuned to "the will of God" (Romans 8:26-27 NRSV). There is a musical exchange going on between the profoundest dimensions of ourselves and the living Spirit of God. It is music because it is beyond speech, and it is mystery because it is beyond sound. Will we acknowledge this sacred harmony and let it shape our lives? Will we let God call the tune?

It is revealing to note that the spiritual seekers of our own generation often talk about wanting to live "in harmony with nature" or "in harmony with things." Harmony is a primal metaphor for aligning our existence with the source and sustainer of all that is. It is a metaphor that works not just across the generations, but across the centuries. Harmony is the metaphor that freed the church to accept music in worship. Harmony is what our own spiritually hungry generation seeks. If the harmony of our lives is to be true and enduring, then it will begin when we allow God to call the tune, when we allow ourselves to attend to the Spirit who even now is singing in our hearts. Listen! Join in!

Thirsting amidst a Flood

Year A, Proper 10: Matthew 13:1-9, 18-23,
Proper 11: Matthew 13:24-30, 36-43, Proper 12: Matthew 13:31-33, 44-52

Does preaching make any difference to the life of this world? By the time we get to church we are already soaked with words. Day by day, minute by minute, words are flooding our lives. Words online. Words on television. Words on radio. Words in our text messages. Words to get us to vote. Words to get us to buy. Words to get us to hate this and love that. Words to nurture product loyalty. Words to appeal to our self-interest. Words to make us feel great about ourselves. Words to get us to question our self-worth. Words, words, words.

Amidst this flood the preacher stands and pours out what? More words! Can preaching possibly make any difference? Will it not be just so many more drops in the ocean of fathomless verbiage?

Sometimes it seems that way to us preachers. Sometimes it seemed that way to Matthew's community. It appeared to them as though proclaiming the good news about the reign of God was futile. All those words that landed on the path where the birds feasted, or on rocky soil, or on land choked by thorns (Matthew 13:4-7), or that got intermixed with weeds (Matthew 13:25)—what difference did those words make? In many cases they made no difference at all. So why did Matthew not give up? Because now and then a word that is *the* word lands in a heart that is hungering for it, that is rich with the desire and the grace and the potential to nurture it and to multiply it far beyond what the preacher could have ever hoped or imagined. Because the word is as necessary to life as leaven is to rising bread (Matthew 13:33), because when you look out at the congregation that has traveled through an ocean of words to arrive in church, they are often as thirsty as the Ancient Mariner: "Water, water, every where, / Nor any drop to drink" (Samuel Taylor Coleridge, "Rime of the Ancient Mariner").

Surrounded by an ocean of words, our hearts and souls still thirst for the word that is life-giving. When the word lands in such a heart, it will yield abundantly, and often in ways that we will never know.

Feasting in a Deserted Place

Year A, Proper 13: Matthew 14:13-21, Proper 14: Matthew 14:22-33

When Jesus heard about John, he withdrew in a boat to a deserted place by himself" (Matthew 14:13). When a lectionary reading starts with a verse like this, I always wonder, what has the lectionary left out?

What had Jesus heard that made him retreat to a lonely place? He had received the news that John had been beheaded and buried. It was John who had prophesied that Jesus would bring the Holy Spirit and fire, John who had claimed he was not worthy to carry Jesus' sandals, and John who had resisted baptizing Jesus until Jesus insisted that he do so. Beheaded. I think of the etchings I have seen of human heads on pikes in Elizabethan England and the news reports of decapitated hostages in our own age. John's beheading must have shaken Jesus to the core of his being. No wonder he got in a boat and set off for a lonely place.

Jesus needed to absorb the shock, to deal with the grief, and to consider the implications of this violent turn of events for his future. But a crowd sees him sailing off in the boat and follows him around the shoreline by foot. Just when he most needs to be alone, he lands amidst a great crowd. He heals the sick and feeds the multitude. But having met their needs, he does not abandon his own. Once the leftovers of the feast are collected, Jesus makes the disciples sail off without him and dismisses the crowd.

Finally, at long last, he goes up a mountain to pray and stays there until very early morning. Did he pray for John and John's family? Did he pray that God would bring an end to Herod's rule? Did he pray for wisdom about what to do next? Did he pray, "Abba, Abba, whatever the future holds, hold me in your hand"? We do not know the content of his prayer. But we do know this: carrying on his urgent ministry amidst a brutal and bloody world, Jesus persisted in finding time to pray. He found in that deserted place enough grace and renewal to press on with his own ministry, including the rescue of his friends from a violent storm upon the lake (Matthew 14:22-33). Perhaps he was able to calm the storm because of the calm granted to him through his time of prayer, because he had feasted in a deserted place on the presence of God.

God's Irrevocable Faith in Us

Year A, Proper 14: Matthew 14:22-33, Proper 15: Romans 11:1-2a, 29-32, Proper 16: Matthew 16:13-20

Have you ever given something to someone and then wanted to take it back? I once gave a rare book to a friend because she was so taken with the volume. Afterwards, I kept pining for that book! My wife got online and eventually found another copy for me.

Sometimes we give something more valuable than a book. We give our trust, our faith, our highest hopes and dreams to others. Then they let us down, and we take back what we gave.

There is a point in this set of readings when Jesus seems on the verge of taking back his trust in the disciples. "You man of weak faith! Why did you begin to have doubts?" (Matthew 14:31). Jesus speaks the words to Peter when the disciple begins to sink while walking on water, but Peter represents all the disciples, including the community for whom Matthew is writing his Gospel. Jesus is in effect addressing his words to the church in every age when its faith begins to wobble.

Nevertheless, Jesus does not withdraw his faith or hope in Peter and the disciples. In a later lection Jesus declares to Peter that he is a rock and "I'll build my church on this rock. The gates of the underworld won't be able to stand against it" (Matthew 16:18). These are astounding words when you consider how fickle Peter and the rest of the disciples prove to be.

Even though Paul the apostle and Matthew the evangelist may never have known each other or each other's writings, there is a striking connection between the Gospel stories of Jesus' willingness not to withdraw his call to the disciples and Paul's theological principle that "the gifts and the calling of God are irrevocable" (Romans 11:29 NRSV). Paul here is working out his understanding of the relationship between the Jews and those who follow Christ. But it would be difficult to find a more accurate summation of the tenacity of Christ in entrusting the gospel to his disciples.

Whenever doubts cloud the conviction that led you to follow Christ, consider afresh these words: "The gifts and the calling of God are irrevocable." Our ministry does not just depend on our faith in God, but God's irrevocable faith in us.

Pardon and Punishment

Year A, Proper 17: Matthew 16:21-28, Proper 18: Matthew 18:15-20,
Proper 19: Matthew 18:21-35

Several years ago there was a notorious news story about "Hockey Dad," who had been sentenced to a maximum term of ten years in prison for manslaughter. Two years earlier, watching his children in an ice hockey game, he felt the coach had allowed things to get too rough. In a fit of rage the Hockey Dad killed the coach.

During the trial there was a period of adjournment when a close relative of the victim met the Hockey Dad in the court hallway and said to him, "I forgive you." Eyewitnesses to the act of forgiveness said the tone was genuine, and there followed a moving exchange between the pardoner and the accused. But on the day of the sentencing, one of the victim's young sons read to the judge an emotional appeal for giving the Hockey Dad the longest possible time in prison. The son's appeal for punishment was as genuine as the pardoner's words of grace. The Hockey Dad received pardon and punishment.

Matthew struggles with pardon and punishment in this month's gospel readings. The command to forgive "seventy-seven times" (Matthew 18:22) follows elaborate directions on how to handle church members who have wronged us (Matthew 18:15-17). If people fail to repent after three attempts at getting them to acknowledge their wrongdoing, then "treat them as you would a Gentile and tax collector" (Matthew 18:17b). That hardly sounds like forgiving seventy-seven times. Likewise, the severity of the punishment given to the unforgiving servant, handing him over "to be tortured until he would pay his entire debt" (Matthew 18:34b NRSV), does not give forgiveness a second chance, let alone seventy-seven chances.

Pardon and punishment: how tangled these issues are in the human heart! Rather than settling for one or the other, Matthew's complex witness affirms that there is room for both in the gospel. By placing these issues in the context of Christ's teaching about his coming crucifixion (Matthew 16:21-28), the evangelist reminds us that we are obligated to approach our decisions about pardon and punishment in a spirit of humility and grace, as followers of one who has both suffered unjustly and forgiven extravagantly.

Balancing Judgment and Grace

Year A, Proper 18: Matthew 18:15-20, Proper 19: Matthew 18:21-35

How do you balance judgment and grace in your daily life? When do you punish your misbehaving child, and when do you decide to let the matter go? When do you call someone to account for a wrong and hurtful action, and when do you decide to release it and move on? When you have erred in your own life, how have you received judgment and grace, whether from someone close to you or from a group? Was the judgment just? Was the grace healing? These are immense questions. They go to the heart of how human communities will preserve some common moral standard while still allowing for the foibles and distortions that are part of our human nature.

There is no single simple principle that in all cases can tell us whether the matter calls for moral judgment or for graciously forgiving and moving on. One of the powerful things about the Gospel readings this month is that they reveal how Matthew's community had a wide range of understandings about judgment and grace.

On the one hand, there is down-to-earth practical advice about calling one another to account for our behavior. The process begins on an individual level and moves onward to involve the entire community (Matthew 18:15-17). According to this passage, offenders are given no fewer than four chances for mending their ways. But if there is no change, no repentance and amendment, the end is judgment and expulsion from the community's graces.

On the other hand, the lection for the next week starts with Jesus' famous admonition that we are to forgive "seventy-seven times" (Matthew 18:22), and the parables that follow reinforce the importance of forgiveness to living the gospel.

A series of sermons could center on this single complex question: How do you balance judgment and grace in daily living? Explore Matthew's varied perspectives on the question, ultimately turning to how God balances judgment and grace in the life and teaching of Christ, our judge and redeemer.

Breaking the Speed Limit
on the Road to Nowhere

Year A, Proper 23: Philippians 4:1-9, Proper 25: Matthew 22:34-46

Having lost our direction, we doubled our speed!" I do not remember the original source of this quotation, but I can still hear the voice of a workshop leader citing the principle. His theme was how human organizations forget the purpose for which they were established.

Automobile drivers may sometimes practice this futile expenditure of effort, but think also of the number of congregations and committees that do the same thing. Becoming vague about the reasons that they exist, they develop busywork. Reports and debates about the least consequential matters increase while significant accomplishment diminishes.

There is in all of us a constant need to reclaim the central purposes for which we were brought into being. Otherwise we lose our direction and double our speed. Our lives become more frantic and less focused. How easily that could have happened to Paul the apostle while he was in prison and writing to the Philippians. He must have been tempted to give in to bitterness and to think only about his sorry state. Perhaps what Paul wrote to the Philippians was a way of reminding himself of what really mattered. Perhaps he was calling himself back to his highest hopes and ideals, for our best sermons are often addressed to ourselves: "If anything is excellent and if anything is admirable, focus your thoughts on these things: all that is true, all that is holy, all that is just, all that is pure, all that is lovely, and all that is worthy of praise" (Philippians 4:8).

In a similar fashion, judging from the internal evidence of his Gospel, Matthew appears to have known the frustration of a church that often lost its way and doubled its energy on the wrong issues. Matthew must have found it salutary to quote Jesus identifying the two greatest commandments and reminding us that *everything* else depends upon them: "All the Law and the Prophets depend on these two commands" (Matthew 22:40).

The next time you are breaking the speed limit on the road to nowhere, stop and listen to the wisdom of Paul and Christ. Get the directions straight before you accelerate.

Silencing Theological Commandants

Year A, Proper 24: Matthew 22:15-22, Proper 25: Matthew 22:34-46

Theology is sometimes reduced to a tricky word game, especially when people are hankering for a good religious fight. I have seen candidates for ordination grilled by individuals who pounce on any statement that in the slightest way suggests something doctrinally spurious. Some people find their identity in being theological guardians, convinced of a divine mandate to protect tradition and orthodox belief. I have witnessed church meetings and seminary classes in which doctrinal absolutes were tossed at opponents like grenades or mortar shells, with the intention of annihilating the other. Instead of drawing us more deeply into the wonder of God, theological conversation can become an acting out of human arrogance, a manifestation of the desire to vanquish others beneath the sanctifying rubric of doing God's will and protecting the faith.

How do we respond to theological commandants eager to confute us? Many of the readings from Matthew this month are instructive because they portray people who, instead of seeking genuine theological dialogue with Jesus, are out to snare him in his own beliefs: "Then the Pharisees met together to find a way to trap Jesus in his words" (Matthew 22:15), and, "When the Pharisees heard that Jesus had left the Sadducees speechless [see Matthew 22:23-33], they met together. One of them, a legal expert, tested him" (Matthew 22:34-35). Jesus refuses to play their word games. His responses leave them "amazed" (Matthew 22:22 NRSV) and "astonished" (Matthew 22:33). In the end he silences their verbal games: "Nobody was able to answer him. And from that day forward nobody dared to ask him anything" (Matthew 22:46).

One way of following Jesus is to silence the theological word games that are not offered in the spirit of mutual enlightenment, of growing in the love and knowledge of God. Our conversational model will be not the theological confrontations of Matthew 22, but the exchange between Jesus and the Samaritan woman in John 4, a conversation that gives glory to God. When we share our disagreements, it must always be in a way that leads us more deeply to the source and core of being, to the eternal God who is so much greater than any of our verbal pyrotechnics.

The Energy Field of Hope

*Year A, Proper 26: Matthew 23:1-12, Proper 27: 1 Thessalonians 4:13-18,
Proper 28: Matthew 25:14-30*

I s life no more than a knitting of cells, an infusion of juice, a brief, bright moment beneath the sun, and then dust scattered by the wind? When Paul the apostle wrote his first letter to the Thessalonians he knew that there were many who held such a view. A tomb inscription from the time reads "I was not; I was; I am not; I care not."[10]

The energy field of hope grows weak when we consider life to be nothing more than damp cells that dry to dust. Paul reminds the Thessalonians of the resurrection so that they "may not grieve as others do who have no hope" (1 Thessalonians 4:13 NRSV). Observe the precision of Paul's language. He does not say, "Do not grieve." Rather our grief is to be different from the grief of those "who have no hope."

For Paul the resurrection reframes grief in configurations of meaning greater than our immediate sorrow. Life is more than a knitting of cells, an infusion of juice, and a brief, bright moment beneath the sun. Our lives are joined to the life of Christ and the hope of resurrection. Because our lives participate in a larger purpose and process, we live in the energy field of hope. That energy field vitalizes the desire to make our lives here and now more congruent with the constellations of eternal meaning manifest in the resurrection.

We no longer live by the values of seeking status (Matthew 23:6-12) or playing it safe with whatever gifts and resources we have (Matthew 25:24-25). These are the strategies of people who take life to be nothing more than a brief knitting of cells that ends in dust dispersed by the wind. For if that is all life adds up to, then it is best to seek fame here and now, best to play it safe so you do not lose the little you have for so brief a time. But if our lives are lived in the hope of Christ, then why waste our energies fighting for status? If we believe in the resurrection, why bury our gifts? Instead, the energy field of hope will move our hearts and minds to risk everything for God.

A Story Line You Can Change

Year A, Proper 27: Matthew 25:1-13, Proper 28: Matthew 25:14-30,
Reign of Christ: Matthew 25:31-46

When I am reading a novel I sometimes turn ahead to the end to see how it will come out, and then, returning to where I left off, I relish tracing all the twists and turns that lead to the end. Other times, I read a book straight through, but when I am finished I go back through earlier scenes and see things I missed before. The end casts the whole story in a different light. Now that it is so easy to watch favorite movies at home, I enjoy the same phenomenon with film. Knowing the end, I almost want to say to the characters as the story is unfolding: "No! Don't do that. Can't you see how this will end?" But it makes no difference. In print or on film, the characters are forever consigned to the same pattern.

Many readings for this month give us pictures of the end of things. A bridegroom shows up when everyone has gone to sleep (Matthew 25:1-13). A financier asks for an accounting of the investments he has entrusted to various staff members (Matthew 25:14-30). The Son of Man makes a final judgment (Matthew 25:31-46). The figures in the parables are as locked into their roles as the characters in the novels and films. But just as I, the reader or viewer of novels and films, am enlightened by the end of the story, so too the endings of the parables set me to examining my life. Things I had forgotten or that had become background now shine in the brighter light that the conclusion of all things provides. I find myself asking, will I be prepared or not for a surprising visit from Christ? Will I be willing to take some risks for the gospel or play things foolishly safe? Will I see that I have been oblivious to where Christ is present among the hungry, the stranger, the prisoner?

We cannot change the story line after we close the covers of the book or watch the last film credit roll by on the screen. But here and now, in the light of the parables of ultimate endings, we are living with a story line that we *can* change.

YEAR B

Extravagant Claims You Can Trust

Year B, Advent 1: Isaiah 64:1-9, Advent 2: Isaiah 40:1-11,
Christmas Day: John 1:1-14

The book of Isaiah makes one extravagant claim after another, and it offers some of the most unconstrained prayers and prophetic pronouncements that have ever been uttered: "If only you would tear open the heavens and come down! / Mountains would quake before you" (Isaiah 64:1). That is not exactly what you would call a timid prayer, a reserved supplication for a modest touch of divine presence. We think our gift lists for Christmas are excessive, but the prophet asks nothing less than an epiphany so global and immense that "the nations would tremble at your presence" (Isaiah 64:2b)!

Or consider the prophet's massive geological language: "Every valley will be raised up, / and every mountain and hill will be flattened" (Isaiah 40:4). I call to mind a vision of the Colorado Rockies where I used to hike and ski. "Every mountain flattened?" I mutter skeptically to Isaiah. The prophet responds in my heart, "Yes, every mountain," for

> Uneven ground will become level,
>   and rough terrain a valley plain.
> The LORD's glory will appear,
>   and all humanity will see it together. (Isaiah 40:4b-5a)

The prophet does not even qualify who will get to see the transformation of earth. You might think the true believers will see it or the righteous will see it or a select company will see it. But no, all people shall see it together.

The church reads these passages from Isaiah as it prepares for the birth of Christ. But look what we end up with: a poor young couple hounded for taxes, a stable, and a baby whose cries mix with the bleating of sheep and the lowing of cattle. Have the mountains moved? Have the heavens parted? Has the wildly extravagant vision of the prophet come true? Before you answer, search your heart for "the true light that shines on all people" (John 1:9). Follow that light to its source, and you will see by its beams the heavens torn apart and the earth transformed. God turns out to be as extravagant as the prophet promised.

Collapsing the Distance between Heaven and Earth

Years A, B, and C, Christmas Day: John 1:1-14

Several years ago near the start of Advent, I awoke to a television report of five people murdered in a fast-food restaurant, and later that same morning I opened my newspaper and read that two robbers had shot a four-year-old girl in the chest when her mother could not silence her crying. My wife and I shook our heads in despair, offered a prayer, and then went on our way to work.

I turned on my e-mail, and the first message told me that a dear friend's brother had been found beaten to death in his office. This time I sobbed. The intensely personal nature of the e-mail message broke open my heart and released the full fury of grief and sadness that had been touched but not mobilized by the morning litany of terror in the news. The distance of the public news stories collapsed beneath the burden of my close friend's agony.

That year I carried all of those brutal killings to the lections for Advent and Christmas, and the weight in my soul compelled me to see the incarnation of Christ in a new way: God in Christ is subjected to the evil and violence of this world. God becomes as vulnerable as the victims in the fast-food restaurant who were found with duct tape over their mouths, as vulnerable as the four-year-old child shot in the chest because she could not stop crying, as vulnerable as my friend's brother beaten in his office. For a moment I stop at the terror of this thought. I pray:

> O Logos, do not become flesh, do not be born of Mary, do not send the angels to the shepherds, do not lay the little child away in the manger. Call it off before it is too late, before you enter this brutal, bleeding world. Stay high and mighty and powerful. Train your troops of angels, train the whole company of heaven and send them swooping down to stop the violence, the terror, the evil.

Then in the silence of my heart I see as never before that incarnation means a refusal to keep a safe distance between heaven and earth, between eternal good and mortal evil. If we are to be godly people we will have to follow the pattern of the incarnation, risking all for love, refusing to keep our distance from the brutality of this world. God is as vulnerable as a child in a stable, as vulnerable as a child in a supermarket whose mother cannot stop her from crying in the presence of robbers. This may not be the all-powerful God we sometimes pray for, but it is the God who becomes flesh to redeem us.

Shaken by Good News

Year B, Epiphany 3: Mark 1:14-20

Sometimes I read through a section of the Bible and the words pass through me as if they were tepid tea, offering neither warmth nor flavor. I get to the end of the passage and realize that I may have gotten the general drift of things, but I have not been struck by the word of God. Whenever this happens, I go back and read the passage aloud because the sound of my voice awakens me to language in a way that reading silently does not. It compels attentiveness to the astounding things that biblical writers often say and that we absorb in the most matter-of-fact manner. This is what happened to me when I read silently, and then aloud, one of the lections for this month: "After John was arrested, Jesus came into Galilee, announcing God's good news" (Mark 1:14). "Arrested" and "good news" in the same short sentence! How can Jesus start preaching good news when the man who baptized him has been hauled off to prison where he will be beheaded at Herod's command (Mark 6:17-29)?

The answer lies in the news that Christ proclaims: the reign of God has come near; it is right here at hand. The reign of God is not some distant paradise but a transforming reality whose possibilities of justice and peace, grace and love are alive in the same world where John is arrested and beheaded, the world of brutal politics and horrific violence that we ourselves inhabit. Therefore, when Christ says, "Repent" (Mark 1:15 NRSV), the word carries the weight of the great prophetic traditions that call not just individuals, but whole peoples and nations to turn around, to change their way of thinking, speaking, and doing. It is usually bad news that shakes us, but Christ brings good news that shakes us.

If we are on this tiny globe in space as just so many vermin fighting each other, our situation is hopeless indeed. But Christ reveals that in truth we are far more than that: we are the beloved creatures of a God whose just and gracious reign is entering this world that we wound and bruise.

The Preacher's Authority in an Age of Suspicion

Year B, Epiphany 4: Mark 1:21-28

There are many titles that historians of the future may give our era, but one that they are certain to consider is "The Age of Suspicion." People are suspicious of political authorities because they have lied so often. People are suspicious of economic authorities because financial markets have collapsed. People are suspicious of religious authorities because they have failed to act swiftly against abuse in the church. People are suspicious of scientific authorities because the products resulting from their discoveries have in many cases devastated the environment.

Preachers feel the loss of authority. I recall a group of older pastors who began their ministries shortly after World War II. Their first congregations granted them significant authority from the day they arrived. But beginning with the mid-1960s, each time they moved to a new pastorate, congregations granted them less initial authority than earlier in their careers. They had to earn authority by proving trust-worthy over time.

In reading Mark, it sounds as though people two thousand years ago were as suspicious of official authority figures as we are: "The people were amazed by [Jesus'] teaching, for he was teaching them with authority; not like the legal experts" (Mark 1:22). One reason for Jesus' authority was his ability to deal with the multiple voices that disrupt human souls: "What have you to do with us, Jesus of Nazareth? Have you come to destroy us?" (Mark 1:24). The authority of Jesus flows not simply from his ability to build rational interpretations of the tradition, but from his power to deal with the forces that fragment human life. The established authorities tried to discredit his gift for bringing wholeness: "He's pos-sessed by Beelzebub. He throws out demons with the authority of the ruler of demons" (Mark 3:22). The authority of our preaching depends in part on how effectively we can give witness to the living Christ whose pres-ence still brings restoration to human lives that have been broken and fragmented. In an age of suspicion, people are hungering for the word that will re-center their being in the deep, dear core of things, the eternal reality of God.

When God Shifts the Paradigm

Year B, Epiphany 4: Mark 1:21-28, Epiphany 6: 2 Kings 5:1-14,
Epiphany 7: Isaiah 43:18-25

There is a trendy phrase in academic circles that provides an arrest-ing slant on this season's readings. The phrase is *paradigm shift*. It describes what happens when new knowledge requires a whole new way of conceptualizing reality. For example, when the idea that the earth was the center of the universe gave way to the scientific work of Galileo and Copernicus, there was a paradigm shift in cosmology.

But paradigm shifts are not limited to science. Transformations of the paradigms in our hearts and heads are common to all of us. We see sev-eral examples of them in the readings for Epiphany. When Jesus exorcises a demon in the synagogue, there is astonishment: "What's this? A new teaching with authority! He even commands unclean spirits and they obey him" (Mark 1:27b). Jesus' teaching was able to reach the troubled depths of the human soul, and those who witnessed it found their usual ideas of teaching and authority inadequate to comprehending what he was doing.

When Naaman the leper was asked to bathe in the Jordan to cure his disease, he was at first affronted by the very idea of such a cure: "Aren't the rivers in Damascus, the Abana and the Pharpar, better than all Israel's waters? Couldn't I wash in them and get clean?" (2 Kings 5:12). Naaman's heart is in his native home, and it is difficult for him to expand the constricted dimensions of his national identity to embrace the healing powers of a foreign land.

When Isaiah (or the prophet writing in his name) announces to the exiles that they will be returning home, he has to deal with the fact that the paradigm that grips the exiles' minds is rooted in the past. God speaking through the prophet tries to break the grip of a past-tense faith:

> Don't remember the prior things. . . .
> I'm doing a new thing;
> now it sprouts up;
> don't you recognize it? (Isaiah 43:18-19)

Helping people see the new thing that God is doing, helping them to shift paradigms, is part of the strenuous work of preaching.

Where Is God Now?

Year B, Epiphany 6: 2 Kings 5:1-14, Epiphany 7: Isaiah 43:18-25

Why is it so difficult for us human beings to find God at work in the world? As a pastor and a teacher in theological education, I have lost track of how many times people have said to me, "Where is God now?" or, "Why can't belief in God today be as simple as it is in the Bible?" The presumption behind this last question crumbles when we turn to the lections for Epiphany 6 and 7. Our readings reveal that people in the Bible often failed to find God at work in the world.

The lection from 2 Kings relates how Naaman, afflicted with leprosy, becomes enraged when instructed by Elisha to wash in the river Jordan, asking, "Aren't the rivers in Damascus, the Abana and the Pharpar, better than all Israel's waters? Couldn't I wash in them and get clean?" (2 Kings 5:12). Damascus is the capital of Aram, Naaman's home, and Abana and Pharpar are his hometown rivers. They are what he is intimately familiar with, and therefore, what he trusts and values. How can some foreign river in a foreign land possibly be the source of healing? If it were not for the skillful intervention of his servants, Naaman might have returned home still afflicted, still wondering where to find God. His prejudice, his cultural bias, his ethnocentricity would have blocked him from acknowledging how God could work in a strange land.

Or consider what Second Isaiah is up against when he tries to get the exiles to see that God is doing something new. Evidently they are still clinging so tightly to past glories that they cannot perceive God moving in the present age:

> Don't remember the prior things. . . .
> I'm doing a new thing;
>   now it sprouts up;
>   don't you recognize it? (Isaiah 43:18-19)

The remembrance of the past, even though it is the remembrance of a sacred past, truncates their theological vision.

Gripping the culture they have always known or fixating on the past they have always honored, people in the Bible sometimes missed the working of God in their present circumstances. I wonder, have you ever encountered that in yourself or your congregation?

The Next Time You Look at a Rainbow

*Year B, Transfiguration Sunday: Mark 9:2-9, Lent 1: Genesis 9:8-17,
Lent 2: Mark 8:31-38, Lent 3: Exodus 20:1-17*

Many years ago the famous actor Orson Welles read from Genesis 9 on the *Johnny Carson Show*: "Never again shall all flesh be cut off by the waters of a flood. . . . When the bow is in the clouds, I will see it and remember the everlasting covenant between God and every living creature of all flesh that is on the earth" (Genesis 9:11-15 NRSV). When Welles finished reading, he preached a one-sentence sermon. These may not be his exact words, but they are close:

"God is not going to destroy us, but it remains to be seen whether or not we will destroy ourselves."

Whenever I see a rainbow in the sky, Welles's sermon returns to me. Like most good sermons, it is true and not true at the same time—for a good sermon never covers all the truth about God, though foolish preachers often make the attempt. Welles's sermon is true because it reminds us of how much trust God has placed in us: whether or not the human race will survive is in our hands. But the sermon is not true because it appears to make God only passive: God will look at the rainbow in the sky and remember not to act against us. But this says nothing about how God will pursue us with grace and love.

Many of the other readings for the season of Transfiguration and Lent take up where Welles's sermon leaves off. God does far more than promise not to destroy us. God persistently supplies us with resources to move from brutality to compassion, from violence to peace. God gives the Law to provide guidance for the moral life (Exodus 20:1-17). God calls us to a new way of being and acting that we can embrace by following Christ (Mark 8:31-38). God provides a transfigured vision of reality so that we can see beyond the long shadows of fear and death to resurrection and new life (Mark 9:2-9). The next time you look at a rainbow, give thanks for the God who not only will not destroy us, but who moves among us so that we might embody the holy vision of a transformed world.

An Extravagantly Unreasonable Way to Live

Year B, Lent 4: John 3:14-21

Sometimes in interpreting why we have acted in a particular way we will say, "I acted in fear" or "I acted in anger" or "I acted in frustration." By describing the state of mind in which we acted, we hope to make sense of our behavior to people who question the reasonableness of what we did. The fear or the anger or the frustration supposedly accounts for our action, reframing it so that it makes more sense not only to others, but to us as well.

Take this principle of explaining our actions and use it to consider the implications of Christ's statement, "Whoever does the truth comes to the light so that it can be seen that their actions were *done in God*"

(John 3:21, emphasis added). Imagine if the explanation for our behavior were not because we acted in fear or anger or frustration, but because we acted in God. What would a life of actions "done in God" look like?

Such a life would not immediately look any more reasonable than actions done in fear or anger or frustration. To love your enemies, to show compassion while living amidst violence, to pray for those who persecute you, to feed the hungry when you are worried about putting food on your own table, to enjoy the company of disreputable outsiders, to live in a way that shows life is stronger than death: these are not actions that appear to be reasonable in a brutal world. To act "in God" rather than out of our instincts for self-survival is an extravagantly unreasonable way to live. Yet it is the very reason we are drawn to Christ. We see Christ consistently acting "in God," so that divine light and truth, love and justice pour through him into the life of the world. Seeing Christ in action, we begin to understand that the most profoundly reasonable actions are not those that we can account for by human psychology, but they are those that are done in the source of every good and perfect gift, done in the spirit of the Word made flesh, done in the womb of being, "done in God."

Did Someone Make You Bear the Cross?

Year B, Palm/Passion Sunday: Mark 15:1-39 (40-47)

Mark's account of the passion of Christ includes this detail: "They compelled a passer-by, who was coming in from the country, to carry his cross; it was Simon of Cyrene, the father of Alexander and Rufus" (Mark 15:21 NRSV). Two words leap out at me: *compelled* and *passer-by*. It sounds like Simon just happened to be at the wrong place at the wrong time. He is not described as someone who was a part of the crowd hungering to see Jesus crucified, nor is he a curious spectator trying to figure out what the hubbub in the streets is about. He is just passing by, out on his own errand, headed for his own destination when without forewarning he is compelled by the Romans to carry Jesus' cross.

The word *compelled* is striking because it is utterly at odds with Jesus' teaching about the cross: "If any want to become my followers, let them deny themselves and take up their cross and follow me" (Mark 8:34 NRSV). There is no compulsion in Jesus' words. Quite the opposite!

Only if people "want" to become followers are they to "take up their cross" (not someone else's cross) and follow Jesus. To *want* to follow Jesus means that you are not a passer-by. You have enough knowledge about Jesus that your desire is to follow him. No soldier or other authority is forcing you to take up the cross.

The distinction between what happens to Simon of Cyrene and what Jesus teaches has pastoral implications for the way preachers speak about the cross. It is essential that we not casually use the phrase *someone's cross to bear*. Those words sometimes function to provide a theological excuse for the burdens that people are compelled to bear that they did not want to take up. I can imagine a sermon or series of sermons based on the question: Did someone make you bear the cross? The question could be a tool for helping people to distinguish their crosses of compulsion from the cross that they bear out of their desire to follow Christ faithfully. The preacher would help people think more precisely about what it means to bear the cross.

A Good Connection

Year B, Easter Eve: Luke 24:13-49, Easter 5: John 15:1-8,
Ascension: Acts 1:1-11

Sometimes I receive a phone call and can barely make out the voice on the other end of the line. I find myself shouting at the top of my lungs, "We've got a bad connection! Hang up and try again!" When we finally get a good connection, our relief springs from something greater than the mechanics and electronics of sound. I believe it is related to the human need to know we are connected, communicating and understanding one another.

The experience of a bad connection is resonant with those deeper breakdowns in communication between human beings and God. This month's Gospel lessons suggest that early church communities had begun to suffer bad connections. If we understand Luke and John to be dealing with the pastoral needs of their communities, then it appears that the Lukan community may have lost touch with the spirit of God or at the very least they had forgotten their dependence upon the Spirit. Luke portrays Jesus commanding: "Stay in the city until you have been furnished with heavenly power" (Luke 24:49). This is such an important theme that Luke will repeat it again at the beginning of Acts: "He ordered them not to leave Jerusalem but to wait for what the Father had promised" (Acts 1:4). Here the analogy between a bad phone connection and our connection with the Spirit breaks down. I can shout over the receiver, "Hang up and try again," but Luke's community will have to wait for the Spirit. There is nothing they can do to compel a good connection.

The situation in John's community appears to be different. Once again there is the importance of a good connection, "apart from me you can do nothing" (John 15:5b NRSV), but this time they are not told to wait. Instead, they are to act in a way that maintains the connection that Christ has established with them: "Abide in me as I abide in you" (John 15:4 NRSV).

When we have a bad connection with the Holy One, we may sometimes wait and sometimes act. The Scriptures wisely show us that both can be faithful responses to restoring communion with God.

Burying the Terror of the Resurrection

Year B, Easter Day: Mark 16:1-8

Death brings comfort as well as grief. Even though there are tears, even though there are things you wish you had said and not said, things you wish you had done and not done, at least you can depend on the finality of death. You have no choice but to make your peace with it.

But what if death is not a reliable absolute? Then the comfort of trusting that life is a fixed and closed system is called into question. If death is overcome, then reality is wide open to possibilities, dimensions, and new worlds that are not ours to possess or command. Break the finality of death and the other finalities of life start breaking as well. No wonder the earliest gospel account of Easter ends not in joy but terror: "Overcome with terror and dread, they fled from the tomb. They said nothing to anyone, because they were afraid" (Mark 16:8).

If we do not stop with Mark's original ending but read all the way to Mark 16:20, then it appears that the early church was not happy with the evangelist's conclusion. Subsequent editors buried the terror of resurrection beneath a pile of extra verses as thick with miracle and promise as the bouquets we bank around a coffin to hide death. The secondary ending to the Gospel is a mirror reversal of Mark's original: "And they went out and proclaimed the good news everywhere, while the Lord worked with them and confirmed the message by signs that accompanied it" (Mark 16:20 NRSV). The new ending transforms the story of resurrection so that it moves from "terror" to "good news," from saying "nothing to anyone" to spreading the word "everywhere."

Perhaps in a way that Mark and his emending editors never intended, the text of the Gospel, as it now stands, tells us something of how we grow into the meaning of the resurrection. We do not grasp the radical nature of the resurrection if all we do is sing, pray, and preach in a joyful and celebratory mode. First we need to know the terror of resurrection. It is a terror to every closed and absolute form of belief. It is a terror to all final and oppressive statements that debilitate our energies to establish a just and compassionate world. If death is overcome, then every force related to death is equally shaky: fear, prejudice, hatred, violence, and all the puny little constructions of meaning and possibility that we have built.

First terror, then joy! First silence, then proclamation! That is the order that emerges at the end of the Mark's emended gospel. It provides a profound homiletical plot for preachers during the season of Easter.

Resurrection Hermeneutics

Year B, Easter 3: Luke 24:36b-48, Easter 5: Acts 8:26-40

Recent decades have seen an explosion in the number of biblical hermeneutics. *Hermeneutic*, coming in part from the Greek messenger god, Hermes, means a particular theory or method of interpreting a text. We are not the first people to generate different ways of interpreting the Scriptures. The early church fervently debated methods ranging from the plain meaning of the text to allegorical, spiritual, and philosophical interpretations.

Many of the lections during Eastertide manifest a "resurrection hermeneutic." They offer interpretations of Scripture that begin with the death and resurrection of Christ. Luke, for example, says of Christ: "He opened their minds to understand the scriptures. He said to them, 'This is what is written: the Christ will suffer and rise from the dead on the third day' " (Luke 24:45-46). The verses are a restatement of what Luke has already presented earlier in the chapter when Christ interprets the Scriptures to the two disciples on the road to Emmaus (24:26).

If we have been trained in historical-critical biblical hermeneutics, we may be wary of using Luke's resurrection hermeneutic because we do not want to fall into the trap of distorting the Hebrew Bible and reading back into its pages what is not there. We know the long history of the church misusing these Scriptures and the resulting evils of anti-Semitism. I believe, however, that it is possible to adapt Luke's resurrection hermeneutic in a way that has integrity for us today.

My theological reasoning goes like this: for Luke's community, Christ was not simply a good religious leader who had been killed. Christ was a living reality known in the breaking of bread and in the believers' ministry among themselves and to others. The risen Christ was the source and center of their being as community, and in the light of the risen Christ they came to know something about God that embraced everything else they knew—including the Scriptures "starting with Moses and going through all the prophets" (Luke 24:27). They realized that God was so great, so good, so compassionate, and so gracious that God would not allow death to be the last word about human life. This realization overpowered all other fine points of interpretation. The ancient Scriptures now shone in their hearts in a way that affirmed as never before the life-restoring character of God. Thus, whether they were preaching to themselves or to outsiders, they interpreted the Scriptures through "the good news about Jesus" (Acts 8:35).

Although we may no longer read the Hebrew Scriptures as did the early church, we still can use a resurrection hermeneutic. We can affirm the utterly astounding character of the life-restoring God who meets us in the Hebrew Scriptures, and who is revealed anew in Jesus Christ, our risen friend who greets us through strangers and who shares bread and wine with us at the table.

Grace Inefficient Is Grace Sufficient

Year B, Easter 4: John 10:11-18

Many years ago a pastor at a workshop told me this story about preparing a sermon on Christ the Good Shepherd. The pastor, who knew nothing about sheep or what it takes to shepherd them, had stumbled upon an article in the city newspaper about a modern-day shepherd who had opened a large sheep operation. The farm was within a reasonable driving distance, so the pastor phoned to ask if he could visit and have a conversation.

The shepherd welcomed the pastor, drove him out into the expansive grasslands where the flocks were grazing, and explained to him the rigors and challenges of raising sheep. One of the most common frustrations was finding lost sheep. When a sheep wandered off, the shepherd got on his cell phone and alerted his fellow shepherds. Each of them then drove a pickup truck around a particular area of the vast grasslands until the animal was found, thrown in the truck, and returned to the flock.

If, however, the same sheep wandered off a second time, it was not returned to the flock. Instead, the creature went straight to the slaughterhouse, because, as the shepherd explained, it takes too many man-hours and too much fuel to keep finding an animal that consistently strays away. Sheep beware: wander twice and the shepherd slaughters you because it is the efficient thing to do!

The grace of the Good Shepherd is the exact opposite. Instead of the wandering sheep getting slaughtered, "the good shepherd lays down his life for the sheep" (John 10:11b). If Christ's grace were efficient, not a one of us would survive. We would get one chance to reform, and that would be it. If grace were efficient, it would not tolerate having to restore us again and again and again to the family of the beloved community. The sufficiency of grace lies in the amplitude of Christ's generosity toward us, a way of being that reveals that efficiency is not the ultimate measure of all things. Thank God that grace inefficient is grace sufficient.

Every Word Matters

Year B, Trinity Sunday: John 3:1-17

When the devil tempts Jesus to command stones to be turned into bread, Jesus responds by quoting from Deuteronomy 8:3: "One does not live by bread alone, but by every word that comes from the mouth of God" (NRSV). Sometimes our preaching gets into a single track, and we effectively settle not for "every word that comes from the mouth of God," but for our personally favorite words that come from the mouth of God. What are your favorite words from the mouth of God? What are your least favorite? Part of what is so appealing about Christ is that he speaks words of judgment and righteousness, words of grace and compassion, with equal authority.

Let us take this principle of living by every word that comes from the mouth of God and apply it to the Gospel reading for Trinity Sunday, John 3:1-17 (Nicodemus), and to John 4:5-42 (the woman at the well). Although the second passage is listed for Lent 3 in year A, this is an example of where we can fruitfully draw upon the longer arc of the gospel narrative that often gets disrupted if we stick too rigidly to the lectionary.

The two stories are close together in John, and they provide dramatic contrasts to one another. Nicodemus on his own initiative approaches Jesus. But Jesus takes the initiative by asking the woman for a drink. Nicodemus comes by night. But Jesus meets the woman at noon. Nicodemus is a respected member of the community. But the community probably marginalizes the woman, judging from her story. Jesus points Nicodemus to the uncontrollable nature of the Spirit using the image of wind. Jesus offers the woman the deep well waters of the Spirit.

Putting these two stories together we can see that every word that comes from the mouth of God tells us that people get to know Christ in different ways. Sometimes it is their questions that bring them to Christ. Sometimes it is Christ who comes to them. Sometimes it happens in darkness, other times in broad day. Sometimes the experience is like the wind in the trees, sometimes it is like water coming up from a deep spring. By preaching every word that comes from the mouth of God, we open our people to the full range of ways that the living spirit of Christ may touch them. Every word from the mouth of God matters.

For All Earth's Storm-Tossed People

Year B, Proper 7: Mark 4:35-41

I have sometimes read a passage of Scripture hundreds of times and missed the same important detail every time. But then one day a phrase that I had never noticed leaps out at me. That happened the last time I read the well-known story of Jesus asleep in the boat as a fierce windstorm arises, and his disciples arouse him with their urgent cry, "Teacher, don't you care that we're drowning?" (Mark 4:38). I have always pictured this as a scene with one lone boat far out from shore, taking waves. I suppose such a reading is the natural result of the earlier verse in which the disciples "left the crowd and took [Jesus] in the boat just as he was" (Mark 4:36a). It sounds as though they left everyone on shore.

But they did not. Mark reports, "Other boats followed along" (Mark 4:36b). Other boats? Apparently, some of the crowd followed in their own boats. People in the other boats would not see Jesus asleep in the stern of his boat, especially when the windstorm came up and their own boats started taking waves.

As a child I used to sail on a mountain lake, and I remember every time a storm came swiftly over the mountain and our boat began taking waves, we started bailing frantically. Nothing else was in our minds except to keep the boat from being swamped. So I picture the crews of all the other boats just as desperate as the disciples in the boat with Jesus but not able to call directly on him. Their boats are going to sink just as quickly as the disciples' boat unless the disciples call upon Christ.

Although Mark may never have intended his passage in this way, I find it a stunning image of the importance of the church asking Christ to still the raging storm. There are boats other than our own that are desperate for Christ's restoring peace. Our prayers of supplication are prayers of intercession for all earth's storm-tossed people.

Ancient Listeners

Year B, Proper 7: Mark 4:35-41

Recalling stories from the past to bring comfort in the present is something that the early church, and particularly the evangelists who wrote our canonical Gospels, knew very well. One way to preach these stories is to imagine the way the evangelists were received by their congregations—to listen to the stories as narrative sermons addressed to the early church.

We do not know all the details of the different communities of faith that gave birth to the Gospels, but we have enough of a picture to form reasonable conjectures about the struggles and threats they faced. In Mark, for example, it may well be that the upheaval forecast in Mark 13 is portraying what his audience was actually already experiencing with the breakout of Christian persecution under Nero. Imagine, then, listeners who know of friends taken away by the authorities. These listeners fear for their own safety (Mark 13:9), and among them are faithful women who are pregnant or nursing children (Mark 13:17). They are people without worldly power, at the mercy of the storms sweeping over them. They huddle together as sisters and brothers in Christ, half wondering why they ever got involved in this movement. Then one of them arises to tell a favorite story, a story that Mark would record as Mark 4:35-41. The familiar plot unfolds: the fleet of boats, the rising storm, Jesus asleep in the stern (as asleep as he seems to be during this time of persecution!), Jesus waking and calming the storm, and then the response of the disciples, "And they were filled with great awe" (Mark 4:41 NRSV). In the telling and hearing of the story, Mark's community perhaps recalled its own sense of awe, and found in that moment of wonder the strength to press on through the violent storms around them. The story calmed their frightened souls as Jesus had calmed the raging seas.

The pattern I have just used for Mark, overhearing the story through the community to whom it was first addressed, is not limited to his Gospel. You can use it with the other evangelists as well. Think of Luke's community wondering if it will have the energy needed to sustain a church whose ministry is now stretching around the perimeters of the known world. What must it have sounded like to hear the story that begins, "When Pentecost Day arrived . . ." (Acts 2:1)? Think of John's community utterly at odds with the established religious and social order.

What must it have sounded like to hear Jesus interceding with God, "I am asking on their behalf . . ." (John 17:9 NRSV)? Listening through those ancient listeners can help us and our own congregations hear the good news as if for the first time.

The Unknowable God Who Calls Us Sister and Brother

Year B, Proper 7: Job 38:1-11, Proper 22: Hebrews 1:1-4; 2:5-12

Have you ever been anxious about how you ought to address someone? Perhaps it was your first job interview or you were traveling abroad or you were meeting someone high up in an organization or you were entertaining someone from an unfamiliar culture. Should you use first names? Should you say Mr., Ms., Doctor, Professor, President, Ambassador, Your Honor? These are not trivial concerns. You feel their weight because you realize that the protocols of decorum give expression to values, assumptions, and understandings that matter a great deal to the building and sustaining of human community.

If you end up getting to know a person well, the way you address each other will often shift as you move from being strangers to friends. I remember when one of my favorite teachers told me as an alumnus, "Call me 'Marie.'" In that moment I realized that she now wanted us to relate as peers, a relationship that would not have been appropriate when she was my professor.

These dynamics of personal interaction give us insight into the range of ways that we relate to God. In the lections for Ordinary Time we see everything from abject awe in the presence of the divine to familiar intimacy. When Job finally encounters God directly, he is in no position to claim that God is a personal buddy:

> Then the LORD answered Job from the whirlwind:
> "Who is this darkening counsel
> with words lacking knowledge?" (Job 38:1-2)

But in the same month's readings we learn that Jesus "isn't ashamed to call [us] brothers and sisters" (Hebrews 2:11). One of the striking things about the biblical witness as a whole is this astounding range of relationships between God and human beings. If our preaching never helps our people encounter the God who is so great, we have no way of responding with anything but awe and humility, and if our preaching never gives witness that Jesus addresses us as members of his family, then it is not true to the unknowable God who calls us sister and brother.

The Gift of Power

Year B, Proper 8: Mark 5:21-43, Proper 12: Ephesians 3:14-21

Power is a word filled with terror. The power of the state can crush individual rights. The power of a bomb can level the city. The power of a mob can silence every voice of protest. "Power corrupts. Absolute power corrupts absolutely" (Lord Acton). Because power is often abused, it is easy to become negative about it, to use power as a synonym for evil and oppression. Living as faithful people then becomes a matter of eschewing power. We reason we must give up on power because it is power that has turned God's creation into a world of conflict and chaos.

But power is also a word filled with wonder and grace. When the bleeding woman in the crowd touches the hem of Jesus' garment he is "immediately aware that power had gone from him" (Mark 5:30 NRSV). When the writer of Ephesians wants to encourage his readers to carry on their ministry boldly, he offers a doxology to God, "who is able to do far beyond all that we could ask or imagine by his power at work within us" (Ephesians 3:20). In both passages the Greek word is the same: *dunamis.* The gospel does not negate power but offers an alternative kind of power: the power to heal, the power to minister, the power "to do far beyond all that we could ask or imagine." The use of this kind of power does not leave one feeling strong and powerful. Just the opposite. When the bleeding woman is healed, Jesus is immediately aware of the loss of power. He knows that power has flowed out of him.

When the power that is at work in us flows out of us, we too are aware of it. Think of those times you have preached the gospel with your whole heart and mind and strength or when some individual or group has profoundly depended upon you. Afterwards, you need to rest. Preachers are famous for taking Sunday afternoon naps! There is more at work here than physiology alone. There is the act of allowing the power of God to work within us and to flow outward as a counterforce to the destructive powers that fill the world.

The Burden of Experience, the Lightness of Trust

Year B, Proper 9: 2 Corinthians 12:2-10

I once had a woman tell me that she was hounded by people in her church about her relationship to Christ because she had never had an experience of the Savior to which she could testify. She told me that she read the Bible, prayed, attended worship regularly, and trusted that somehow, in a way beyond her comprehension, Christ is with us. But she could not point to any conclusive encounter with Christ, any experience in which she felt she directly apprehended the divine. She would like to have had such an experience, and she believed others had such experiences, but if it never happened to her, she would settle for simply trusting Christ because that seemed to be all that Christ required.

Her story raises a profound issue: what is the place of religious experience in the life of faith? Some believers undergo a numinous encounter with the Holy, the risen Christ, the ineffable One, or however they name God. Such an experience is so revelatory and transformative that it becomes for them the test of faith not only for themselves, but also for others. Evidently something like this perspective prevailed among some believers in Corinth. Paul's credentials as an apostle may have been called into question for lack of such testimony on his part, and so he concludes that "it is necessary to brag" about his experience (2 Corinthians 12:1-4), although he is quick to add "not that it does any good," and once he is finished with his testimonial he reflects, "I've become a fool! You made me do it" (2 Corinthians 12:11).

One way to read Paul is to dismiss his repudiation of the importance of experience as a rhetorical strategy: he is eager to share his experience but does not want to appear boastful. But another reading is that Paul is deadly serious about the matter. He really is opposed to sharing extraordinary religious experience as the standard of faith because he knows how easily the sharing of experience might turn into a competition: I've had a bigger and better experience of God than you! I wonder, do our sermons affirm the lightness of trust or the burden of experience?

The Cavernous Realm of Inner Voices

Year B, Proper 10: Mark 6:14-29

What do people hear when you preach? They hear your voice and your words, the inflections and pauses that make up the music of speech—the ideas, images, and stories that you tell. But they also hear something else, not with the ear but with the heart. They bring to your words the fears and joys that are alive in their souls and that the language and symbols of worship give them permission to acknowledge. From the deep, cavernous realm of inner voices arise anxiety and confusion, hope and clarity.

The encounters between John the Baptist and Herod give witness to how complex the relationship of the preacher's voice and the listeners' inner voices can be. On the one hand, Herod respects John. The king knew "that he was a righteous and holy man, and he protected him," yet Herod's response to his preaching appears to be a mixture of confusion and fascination: "When he heard him, he was greatly perplexed; and yet he liked to listen to him" (Mark 6:20 NRSV), or as J. B. Phillips paraphrases the situation, "He used to listen to him and be profoundly disturbed, and yet he enjoyed hearing him." At some deep level, John the Baptist's preaching hooked Herod, even though John minced no words about the wrongness of Herod's marriage to his brother's wife. Whatever went on in Herod's soul when he heard John preach, it continued to haunt him after John's death. When Jesus' reputation began to spread, the king said: "John, whom I beheaded, has been raised" (Mark 6:16).

This tangled story of preacher and king, of fascination and disturbance, reminds us that preaching, especially preaching to the powers of this world, involves us with far more than the rational mind. Preaching can reach into the quagmire of the soul, sometimes with disastrous results— John got beheaded. But because preaching can reach the troubled depths of human existence, it also holds the promise of human transformation. I wonder what might have happened to Herod if he had not made a rash promise to his dancing daughter. Might the disturbance and fascination of John's preaching have led in time to Herod's repentance? Perhaps not. But who knows at what deep level your preaching may remake a life?

Conspiracies Worth Knowing About

Year B, Proper 10: Ephesians 1:3-14

There is something in the human psyche that feeds on the thought of conspiracy.[1] Sometimes it is mere projection, but there are other times when there is in fact a conspiracy, a network of secret planning and covert operations that can overthrow a government or fly airplanes into tall buildings. These are the conspiracies that grab the headlines and grip the heart with fear. They speak to the most shadowed and frightened parts of who we are. They disrupt and corrode the qualities of trust and communication in the human community, and if they are the only hidden realities at work in the world, then we are in profound trouble. We had better know about such conspiracies if we want to survive.

But there is another kind of hidden reality—the profound workings of God—that transforms human life. The author of Ephesians gathers these gracious dynamics together under the grand general phrase "the mystery of [God's] will" (Ephesians 1:9 NRSV). This mystery—a conspiracy of grace and love and hope—is working to displace the conspiracies that awaken fear and disrupt trust and communication among us human beings. We had better know about this conspiracy if we want to do more than survive—if instead we want to thrive with abundant life.

Destructive conspiracies sometimes erupt in violent acts, and the divine conspiracy, the mystery of grace and love and hope, also sometimes erupts at certain revelatory moments, becoming brilliantly manifest in human life. The beginning of the Gospel of Mark gives witness to this through the baptism of Jesus and the calling of Simon and Andrew (Mark 1). John the Baptist was ready when the bearer of the divine conspiracy came before him in the person of Jesus. Simon and Andrew responded when they sensed the mysterious working of God calling them from their nets and boats, and the result was the eternal transformation of who they were and what they did. With the continuing focus upon conspiracies of terror and fear, will we lose our receptivity to the working of God for goodness, truth, and justice? Our task as preachers in these days is not to let the knowledge of this holy mystery slip from our people's hearts.

A Transition of Power

Year B, Proper 12: John 6:1-21

The Gospel writers often tie stories together with a very brief transition. For example, between the miracles of Jesus feeding the multitude and Jesus walking on water, the evangelist inserts a single verse: "Jesus understood that they were about to come and force him to be their king, so he took refuge, alone on a mountain" (John 6:15). Although it is an intriguing bit of information, John appears to use the verse as little more than a transition from one miracle to another.

The miracle stories picture Jesus as someone of extraordinary power. Yet Jesus evidently does not have the power to overcome those who would "force him to be their king." We might reasonably expect that someone with his gifts would not have to retreat from those who want to elevate him to a position of political and social prominence. If he can feed five thousand people with a child's lunch and walk across a storm-tossed sea, surely he can quiet a crowd that is at cross-purposes with him. But to think this way is to misunderstand Jesus and the character of his action.

The transitional verse is a commentary on the two miracle stories that helps us to grasp more profoundly the nature of Jesus' power. His retreat from those who would make him king shows us that the character of his power is different from what the crowd thinks.

The two miracles speak to the deepest needs of the human body and soul: food and peace. Christ's capacity to meet these needs arises not from the kind of "force" that the people would use to coronate him, but rather from the integrity of his relationship to God, a relationship suggested by the words "he took refuge again, alone on a mountain." Mountains are traditionally a place of prayer and epiphany in the Scriptures. Returning to the source that empowered him to feed the multitude, his powers will be renewed. The verse that initially seemed a digression in the narrative turns out to be a revelation that calls the world to a transformed understanding of power.

Getting the Heart in Shape

Year B, Proper 14: John 6:35, 41-51, Ephesians 4:25–5:2

What makes for a healthy heart? If by heart we mean the valved, four-chambered muscle that pumps blood through our arteries, there is a litany intoned by the priests of health:

- Eat a diet high in fiber and low in saturated fats.
- Avoid too much stress.
- Exercise regularly.

If, however, by heart we mean the spiritual core of who we are as individuals and communities, then our culture becomes much less knowledgeable and articulate about what makes for a healthy heart. We are not unlike the people who appear in the Gospel readings for John this month. They know what they need physically—"You are looking for me not because you saw miraculous signs but because you ate all the food you wanted" (John 6:26)—but they miss what they need spiritually. Although our age appears obsessed with finding something that it vaguely calls *spirituality*, the search often has a frenetic, faddish character to it.

In order to keep the heart healthy, John the evangelist offers a steady diet of eucharistic worship—of regularly feeding upon Christ in the community of faith. Expressing the desire of the congregation for whom he writes, John puts words into the mouth of the crowd: "Sir, give us this bread all the time" (John 6:34).

John's first principle for a healthy heart parallels what we know about the physical heart: keep to the right diet. Feed upon Christ. But since Communion is a community act, John makes clear that a healthy spiritual heart is not something we acquire on our own. Communion is not fast food picked up at a drive-through window and wolfed down as we speed frantically to our next appointment. The need to feed upon Christ in a community of faith is analogous to the second condition for a healthy physical heart: a haven from stress where the heart can relax. Such community was especially important to John's congregation because they were under constant stress from a world that was at odds with their belief and practice.

The writer of Ephesians affirms the third principle for a healthy heart, the need for exercise: "Walk in love, as Christ loved us" (Ephesians 5:2

ESV). *Walk* is translated *live* in the NRSV, but I prefer the literal translation of the Greek *peripateite*, from which we get *peripatetic*. Exercise the way Christ did: walk in love.

Since these readings occur during summer for lectionary followers, a time when many people are out jogging, hiking, playing tennis, golfing, or swimming, use your sermons to deepen and expand the meaning of their physical activity. Imagine if every time your people went out to exercise it occurred to them to think of this litany for a spiritually healthy heart:

- Feed on Christ.
- Participate in the community of Christ.
- Walk in love, as Christ loved us.

Boundless Thanks

Year B, Proper 17: James 1:17-27

I have often noticed in worship services that when the congregation is invited to offer their prayers aloud, the number of supplications far exceeds the number of thanksgivings. Not infrequently, a long series of pleas for help will be followed by utter silence when the liturgist calls for prayers of thanks.

One of the lections from James this month has a beautiful phrase of gratitude that I learned as a child in the King James Version: "Every good gift, every perfect gift, comes from above" (James 1:17a). What would it be like if we were to offer unlimited thanks to the source of every good and perfect gift? I find this an interesting spiritual exercise. Every now and then I try it and discover that by the time I finish thanking God, I have a sense that my profoundest supplications are already being addressed.

> *Thanks be to you, O source of every good and perfect gift, for breath and pulse and life and sun and sky and moon and stars and trees and the Handel flute sonatas and love and friendship and work and rest and sleep and waking up and energy and my wife and the way the ground feels beneath my feet and the grace of Christ that comes through strangers and the challenge of trying to understand the Scriptures and the times I have known reconciliation and*

peace and the smell of broom plants blooming in the garden and snow and rain and dry air and the shadows of clouds playing on mountains and the riches of different cuisines and music and dance and art and beauty and the grain of wood and the heft of stone and the multitudinous ways humanity names you and the delight of arriving home at night and the way you keep engaging my heart yet eluding all the ways I try to contain and define you so that I find myself continually opening to realities and thoughts and dreams that hint at your own great wild imagination that conceived of a billion billion stars yet still remembered this little whirling watered stone to which you sent Jesus Christ in whose name I pray. Amen.

Truth in Preaching

Year B, Proper 17: Mark 7:1-8, 14-15, 21-23, Proper 19: James 3:1-12

I magine if you were to go into a supermarket and every package were the same brown cardboard color, and the words describing the contents were all in the same typeface. You would look down aisle after aisle and see nothing but walls of the same dull cardboard. It would take you a long time to find precisely what you wanted.

Now switch from that imagined scene to what you actually find when you step into a supermarket: aisle after aisle of brilliantly colored packages, their brand names inseparable from the script in which they are written. If the product is a staple in your home, you do not even have to stop to read the packaging. You know what it looks like and you can find it amidst all the competing brands. The package announces the contents. When you open it, you know what will pour out.

Even though we human beings are not monochromatically packaged creatures, it is much more difficult to tell what lies in our hearts on the basis of our appearance. Sometimes how we look gives us away: the body hunched in despair, the eyes shining with delight, the mouth drawn tight in fear, the spring in our step after receiving great news. Most of us can read these signs, especially in those we love.

But the enduring contents of the heart are not instantly available to us. They only become evident through the behavioral patterns of a lifetime, and these are the contents that concern Jesus in Mark 7 and James, who uses some striking metaphors to stress the need for spiritual integrity, for congruence between our inward being and our outward action (James 3:11-12).

How splendid it would be if our actions matched what we boldly claim to believe, if the world found in the life of the church the grace and love that our prayers and sermons promise. Imagine a church whose fellowship and mission were every bit as nourishing and satisfying as the gospel it proclaims. That would be more than truth in advertising. It would be truth in preaching.

The Breaker and Maker of Taboos

Year B, Proper 17: Mark 7:1-8, 14-15, 21-23, Proper 18: Mark 7:24-37, Proper 19: Mark 8:27-38, Proper 20: Mark 9:30-38

I remember the taste of brown soap. It always nearly made me vomit, which is why my mother used it to wash my mouth out after she had caught me using bad words.

My parents made it clear that there were certain taboos, words not to be used, topics not to be discussed. They were not always related to "dirty" language. For example, I once asked a question about death in the presence of my father and his aging parents. My father made it clear that this was inappropriate. It was a taboo.

My experience is not unique. All cultures, all human cultures have taboos that make clear what is not acceptable language or behavior. Different churches have different taboos, and savvy pastors quickly discover what they are. "We don't talk about that here." "We do the sacrament this way." Challenging a taboo can be dangerous. It will usually appear as a threat to the values and structures of a community.

I am indebted to some lectures by the New Testament scholar David Rhoads for making me aware of how significant taboo and the breaking of taboo are to the way Mark presents Jesus. Again and again in Mark we encounter actions and words that manifest the power of taboo and the community's resistance to breaking them. The religious authorities call Jesus to account for not requiring that his disciples practice the ritual washing of hands (Mark 7:1-5). Peter tries to establish his own taboo against Jesus talking about his coming suffering and death (Mark 8:31-33). And a Syrophoenician woman helps Jesus himself overcome the powerful taboos that separate Jews and Gentiles, men and women, in order to heal her daughter (Mark 7:24-30). If Jesus had not broken the taboo, he would not have been able to respond to the woman and restore her child.

There are taboos that need to be broken and taboos that need to be kept. A world without any taboos would be a world without any moral values. Jesus challenges taboos that oppress and exclude people, but he also establishes other taboos. For example, he makes it clear to Peter that not to talk about his suffering and death is to violate the realism of true faith that squarely faces the tragic and painful character of human existence (Mark 8:33). Likewise, Jesus has a taboo against the world's usual hierarchies of power, and the disciples must have known this because "they were silent" when Jesus asked about a conversation in which they had debated who was the greatest (Mark 9:33-37 NRSV).

Talk to your congregations about taboos: what taboos have we lost, what taboos have we established, what taboos are destructive, and what taboos are life enhancing? These are questions that flow from Christ, the breaker and maker of taboos.

Something in the Human Heart

Year B, Proper 19: Mark 8:27-38, Proper 20: Mark 9:30-38

There is something in the human heart that does not want to face up to suffering and death. Mark the evangelist knew this. If I were to provide a subtitle to his work I might call it *The Gospel of Mark: How the Suffering and Death of Jesus Transform Our Understanding of Suffering and Death.*

From the moment Jesus announces that "the Son of Man must undergo great suffering" (Mark 8:31 NRSV), he meets resistance. Peter, speaking for all of us, tries to silence such talk, and Jesus responds: "Get behind me, Satan!" (Mark 8:33). But this does not end the disciples' resistance and their failure to understand. After the transfiguration, the theme returns again, and this time, although no one attempts to hush Jesus, there is a kind of silent resistance that is based on the disciples' fear: "But they didn't understand this kind of talk, and they were afraid to ask him" (Mark 9:32).

Mark presents Jesus' life and passion in a way that transforms our natural human resistance to facing the harsh realities of suffering and death.

Instead of becoming philosophical or appealing to our reason, Mark interweaves the story of Jesus with the disciples' balking at predictions of his death. We watch as Jesus faces the truth, and as the inexorable momentum of events reveals the futility of Peter's and the disciples' refusal to come to terms with these cruel realities. They and Mark's original readers would have preferred a more Greek-like divine figure, a changeless deity who stands above the pain and hurt of this world. Instead, Mark shows them Jesus, who knows he will suffer and makes no attempt to hide it. The disciples will be baffled until after the resurrection when they discover that it is through such profound identification with the pain, death, and injustice of the world that the glory of God emerges triumphant. If we open ourselves to Mark's severe but honest vision, then the passion and resurrection of Jesus will overcome that something in the heart that would rather turn away from the brutalities of this world. The resurrection gives us strength to face life as it actually is.

Act Before You Preach

Year B, Proper 21: Mark 9:38-50

Do words give birth to actions or do actions give birth to words? As preachers, we put great stock in words, and we deliver sermons hoping and trusting that words will give birth to actions. Often they do! I can think of many a sermon I have heard that was far more than a fountain of speech evaporating in the air. Each was the impetus that stirred me to faithful and compassionate action. But the opposite is also true: actions give birth to words.

Here is a striking instance of how faithful actions have the potential to lead to faithful speech: John is upset because someone who is not a member of the circle of disciples is casting out demons in Christ's name. The teacher's reply is generous and wise: "Don't stop him. No one who does powerful acts in my name can quickly turn around and curse me" (Mark 9:39).

Names had extraordinary importance in the ancient world. To do something in someone's name was to invoke their essential character, the peculiar power of their being. When the exorcist healed someone in Christ's name, the power of Christ was released both upon the one whose demon was cast out and upon the exorcist. Acting in the power and pattern of Christ had consequences for the exorcist's speech. She or he (Mark does not specify the gender) would not be able to speak ill of Christ, and most probably would begin to speak positively of the one whose name had been embodied in an act of compassion. Action would give birth to word.

Here then is another way to find words for a sermon: act before you preach.

Let your action give birth to language. In the name of Christ, forgive. In the name of Christ, reconcile. In the name of Christ, do justice. In the name of Christ, stand with someone who is grieving or rejoicing. In the name of Christ, feed the hungry. Then see what words emerge out of the action. Not only will you not speak ill of Christ, but I believe you will preach with renewed vitality the wonder of Christ.

Headed in Opposite Directions

Year B, Proper 22: Mark 10:2-16, Proper 23: Hebrews 4:12-16,
Proper 24: Mark 10:35-45

I was once trying to find someone at the airport, and the two of us later discovered that when I had been riding up the escalator, he had been riding down the escalator. This must have happened two or three times, until at last we just happened to see each other as I was riding up yet again and he was riding down. We waved wildly, and he shouted, "I will wait for you on the ground floor!"

God and human beings are often headed in opposite directions. We creatures of dust keep hankering to rise up to a position of higher prestige and power. James and John ask Jesus: "Allow one of us to sit on your right and the other on your left when you enter your glory" (Mark 10:37). Meanwhile, God in Christ identifies with our human condition: "Because we don't have a high priest who can't sympathize with our weaknesses but instead one who was tempted in every way that we are, except without sin" (Hebrews 4:15). We are headed up and God is headed down, and sometimes we miss each other just as my friend and I kept missing each other.

How are we going to make connections with God if we keep heading in opposite directions? That to me is a much more fruitful question than,

"Does God exist?" While this second question leads through endless con-volutions of thought, the first question suggests something we can actu-ally do: we can choose to stop heading up; we can choose to accept our humanity and finitude, to live with who and what God has made us to be. We can reclaim the capacity for wonder and astonishment at the world that we once had as children (Mark 10:14-15).

Our world is going through a period of frantic, anxious searching, much of it religious in nature, and that inevitably involves collisions between different faiths and theologies. Rather than argue about God in the abstract and whose belief is true or false, perhaps we as a community of creatures could begin with the simple affirmation: we are all human. We might then be startled to realize God is here among us, sharing in our common humanity.

My Teacher, Let Me See Again

Year B, Proper 22: Mark 10:2-16, Proper 23: Mark 10:17-31,
Proper 24: Mark 10:35-45, Proper 25: Mark 10:46-52

In Mark 10, Jesus turns the world of good religious people upside down. All of their assumptions about how the world is supposed to work crumble. They assume the law of Moses, the very law of God, is ulti-mate and inviolable. But the law turns out to be inadequate when it comes to the question of divorce, because it was written for humanity's "hardness of heart" (Mark 10:5 NRSV). The good religious people assume that the world of theology is too serious an adult matter to be disrupted by children. But Christ demolishes their presumption by commanding: "Allow the little children to come to me" (Mark 10:14). They assume that the rich have it made. But that commonly held belief bites the dust as Christ announces, "It's easier for a camel to squeeze through the eye of a needle than for a rich person to enter God's kingdom" (Mark 10:25). They assume, like the sons of Zebedee, that unless people demand a posi-tion of prestige and power they will never achieve it. But Christ disarms their strategies and maneuvers for privilege: "Whoever wants to be great among you will be your servant. Whoever wants to be first among you will be the slave of all" (Mark 10:43).

It is clear from the disciples' behavior—James and John requesting prime seats in the kingdom and the anger they stir among the others—that it is not easy for good religious people to give up their assumptions and see the world as Christ does. And if we are honest about ourselves, we are not very different from them. Their assumptions and ours are close if not the same. Just look at how we live. We appeal to the law rather than acknowledge the hardness of our hearts. We adults too often discount the wonder and wisdom of children. We live as though we can buy security. The race to the top goes on in every field of human endeavor. When the world appears to prevail, how will we ever see the reign of God disrupting our assumptions?

Mark answers the question by finishing the chapter with the healing of Bartimaeus. Knowing full well that he is blind, Bartimaeus asks Jesus, "Teacher, I want to see" (Mark 10:51). Perhaps we need to acknowledge that we too are blind, praying, "My teacher, let me see again; let me see the reign of God that crumbles my assumed world."

Optometry for the Human Heart

Year B, Proper 24: Psalm 104:1-9, 24, 35c

I will never forget when, in third grade, I received my first pair of glasses to correct my nearsightedness. I had no idea the world could look so clear and sharp. The ends of bare tree branches were no longer a blur. I could trace every twig and where they met the slender branches and where the slender branches met the thick branches and where the thick branches met the trunk. It was a miracle—or so it seemed to me! Corrective lenses turned a blurred world into a clear world, a world that astounded me with a depth and complexity that I never knew was there until I put on those glasses.

Preaching is optometry for the human heart. We know in a vague way that there is something wonderful and mysterious about the elemental fact of existing, but preaching clarifies our blurry human perception, helping us see the depth and complexity that we otherwise miss. The writer of Psalm 104 provides a model for how this spiritual refraction takes place.

Verses 1-23 are filled with vivid descriptions of the created world that are typical of a naturalist's attention to the details of landscape and habitat:

> The stork has a home
>> in the cypresses.
> The high mountains
>> belong to the mountain goats;
>> the ridges are the refuge of badgers. (Psalm 104:17b-18)

But then the psalmist pushes beyond the materiality of the world to the source of all that lives:

> When you let loose your breath,
>> they are created,
>> and you make the surface of the ground brand-new again.
> (Psalm 104:30)

Just as putting on glasses refocuses the world, so too the psalmist's theological reflection upon creation intensifies and clarifies our sense of wonder till it bursts into worship: "But let my whole being bless the LORD! / Praise the LORD!" (Psalm 104:35b).

One purpose of preaching is to provide corrected vision—to help our hearers gain a perceptiveness to realities that otherwise elude our awareness. The process of spiritual refraction is what allows us to "see God's kingdom," and the name of that process is "being born from above" or "born anew" (John 3:3).

What Comes First?

Year B, Proper 26: Mark 12:28-34

I consume large quantities of sticky notes to remind me of things I need to do, though in recent years computerized lists have augmented these. Whether I use paper or electronic reminders, the hope has remained the same: that I would not become overwhelmed by the sheer amount of stuff to do! That I would get organized and get things written down so I don't forget them.

Sooner or later the lists become unmanageable. I have to tear down the notes plastered to the walls about my desk or hit the delete button on the computer. But first I cull through them and decide which ones matter most. Sometimes that is a difficult task because there are several items that matter a great deal, and yet I must prioritize. I have to decide that some things are in fact much more important than others.

From talking with many friends and colleagues, I find that my behavior is not idiosyncratic. We all have some way of trying to organize our lives, and whatever our system may be, there are periodically times when we need to examine and review, often asking: what is most important?

"Which commandment is the most important of all?" a scribe asked Jesus (Mark 12:28). A scribe was someone who knew the law thoroughly, who honored the law as a gracious gift from God that gives life meaning and order and direction. Yet even the scribes had a need to prioritize, to get clear what comes first, what is central to all of human existence. Without this clarity, the law—even though it is a gift from God—can become as impenetrable as my wall plastered with sticky notes or my computer filled with lists.

Our souls and hearts are just as susceptible to clutter and confusion as our weekly schedules, so we must periodically get back to the core, back to the center. I believe it is this process of clarifying and centering upon essentials that lies behind the Shaker hymn, " 'Tis the Gift to Be Simple." Notice the hymn does not say, "Tis the gift to be simplistic." *Simplistic* means ignoring the inevitable complexity of life. But being *simple* means finding the clarity that helps us to negotiate the complexity of life with grace and kindness.

We become simple when we realize that the first and great commandment is, "Hear, O Israel: the Lord our God, the Lord is one; you shall love the Lord your God with all your heart, and with all your soul, and with all your mind, and all your strength" (Mark 12:29-30 NRSV).

The commandment is not spoken to an isolated individual, but rather to the community of faith: *Hear, O Israel.* The form of the commandment is liturgical: it is a call to communal worship. This is significant because it reminds us that spiritual simplicity is achieved not by the individual in isolation, but by the community at prayer. Being in community reminds us that it is never adequate simply to get our individual lives in order, but rather it involves the ordering of our mutual existence.

The next time you are reviewing your sticky notes or cleaning out your computer lists—or whatever it is you do to organize your life—pause for

a minute before you begin, and remember the two greatest commandments: love of God and love of neighbor. It will help in deciding all your
other priorities, and you will then be, as Jesus says to the scribe, not "far
from God's kingdom" (Mark 12:34).

A Penny's Worth of Galaxies

Year B, Proper 26: Mark 12:28-34, Proper 27: Mark 12:38-44,
Reign of Christ (Last Sunday after Pentecost): Revelation 1:4b-8

Articles about the cosmos always catch my interest. I cannot claim
to understand every astrophysical explanation, but I am always
filled with astonishment when I read about light that began to
travel toward earth before the planet even existed. That same sense of
wonder returns to me when I am skiing down the Continental Divide
from an elevation of 13,000 feet. I marvel at the massiveness and age of
the alpine peaks that surround me. Then suddenly it hits me: I am
impressed with these awesome peaks, and yet they are nothing more than
wrinkles on a little stone that revolves around a minor star in a galaxy
that is only one among fifty billion galaxies.

The discrepancy in size between my little world and the cosmos is the
same scale of realities we find in our lections as we approach the end of
Ordinary Time in the lectionary year. We read that time itself is encom-
passed by "the Alpha and the Omega" (Revelation 1:8). But we also
observe the smallest act of giving: "One poor widow came forward and
put in two small copper coins worth a penny" (Mark 12:42). Between the
beginning and end of time, a widow gives a penny to the temple treasury,
and Jesus is so moved by her action that you might conclude it is one of
the major events in the history of the cosmos.

That is exactly what the widow's gift is.

The tiniest act of generosity, when it is a giving of one's whole self,
commands a holy place in creation, in the unfolding of God's purposes
and the fulfillment of God's reign. The God who is stoking the fires of
fifty billion galaxies, the God who encompasses all of time, rejoices at a
widow who gives a penny as an act of faith and worship. By putting everything she has into the temple treasury (Mark 12:44), the widow embodies the greatest commandments (Mark 12:28-34). Her action is an event

in the stream of time that is in harmony with the source and goal of time, "the Alpha and the Omega." Who knows what act of love you and I have received as a result of that widow's generosity centuries ago? Love travels across time as surely as the light that set out for earth before earth existed.

Whenever you grow weary preaching and wonder if it matters that you spend so much time and effort to find the best way to speak the word of God to your people, go outside some clear night and look at the stars. Then look down deep and you may rediscover the passion that first drove you to preach: an irrepressible desire to give to the treasury of God your penny of faith and love, a penny worth a thousand galaxies.

Perplexed by Christ the King

Year B, Reign of Christ: John 18:33-37

The Apostles' Creed affirms that Christ "suffered under Pontius Pilate," and the Nicene Creed recounts how Christ "was crucified under Pontius Pilate." Even if you do not come from a creedal tradition, imagine how many billions of times these phrases have been uttered by Christians through the centuries. I wonder what Pilate would say to this. Would he even remember? Crucifixion was standard practice for enforcing Roman occupation. Sending Jesus off to be crucified may have been no more memorable for Pilate than reading an accountant's report or signing a requisition form. Torture and death were part of the job, and when something is routine, it is difficult to recall discrete actions. Hearing his name recited in the creed, Pilate might ask: "Which execution are you talking about?"

Or perhaps not. Perhaps Pilate would remember. According to John's account, Jesus left the Roman bureaucrat perplexed. When Jesus explains the nature of his reign, Pilate responds, "So you are a king?" (John 18:37), and when Jesus says that he has come to give witness to the truth, Pilate again responds with a question, "What is truth?" (John 18:38). Pilate would most probably have forgotten the suffering he caused Jesus, but he might well remember how that Galilean left him pondering the nature of government and truth. Instead of "suffered under Pontius Pilate," the Roman ruler might wonder why the creeds do not recall how he had been "perplexed by Jesus Christ."

It is easy to judge Pontius Pilate, especially since the creeds have assured him an enduring infamy, but John's text suggests that Pilate is more than simply the bad guy who handed Jesus over to the executioners. Pontius Pilate, the perplexed, reminds us that one of Christ's many roles—and one of the functions of Christian preaching—is to leave us baffled, to make us question all of those facile certitudes and routine procedures whose deeper consequences we have never considered. Our homiletical structures need to be clear, but the impact of our preaching should be to raise disturbing questions that loosen the grip of the violence and brutality that find their way into nearly every system of human governance.

Belonging to Christ

Year B, Reign of Christ: John 18:33-37

Have you ever taped your name to the back of a casserole dish that you brought to a potluck supper or onto the handle of a rake you brought to a community-wide clean-up-the-park day? You wanted to be sure you got that dish or the rake back. You owned it and it had your name on it because you did not want to lose it.

When something belongs to us, we invest more than just the money it took to purchase. We invest a sense of ownership in it and sometimes even a special meaning and value, as for example, "That casserole dish was the first thing I bought with our wedding gift money. I still remember the first meal I cooked in it—the first time I brought it from the oven to our table."

But imagine the situation in reverse: not something that belongs to you, but someone or some group to whom you belong, as in belonging to a lifetime partner or to a church or to God. Unlike a casserole dish or rake, you are conscious of belonging to another, and the relationship is not simply one way, as it is with an inanimate object. You cannot use the one to whom you belong any way you wish, any time you wish. You have to be attentive to the other to whom you belong.

Christ draws on the complexity of belonging to another in responding to Pilate's questions: "Whoever accepts the truth listens to my voice" (John 18:37). Pilate belongs to Caesar, not to the truth, and he must listen to Caesar or at least to what he reasonably believes Caesar would expect him to do with an expendable victim whose execution will avert a mob from rioting in the streets.

Since Christ is the truth, it follows that if we belong to the truth, we listen to Christ's voice. What a profound way to understand preaching! We often talk about what it takes to create a sermon, and of course, there is much hard preparation on our part in order to preach the gospel faithfully. But that process needs to be embedded in something more profound. It needs to flow from our belonging to Christ and listening to Christ's voice.

What the Spirit Is Saying to the Churches

Year B, Reign of Christ: Revelation 1:4b-8

Whenever I hear sermons about the call of God to ministry, they are usually about a call to an individual. Sometimes the sermon gives witness to the preacher's own call. Other times, it may be a story about someone in the Bible or in history who was called to a particular ministry. Many of these sermons have been rich with insight and wisdom.

But seldom have I heard a sermon about the call of God coming to an entire community.

Yet the book of Revelation features what the spirit of the Risen Christ is saying to the churches of Asia (modern-day Turkey). The passage for what is known as the Reign of Christ (Revelation 1:1-8) points ahead to these edicts, and it would, therefore, make good sense to build them into a sermon or perhaps a series of sermons.

Again and again in chapters 2 and 3 we read the commandment: "Let anyone who has an ear listen to what the Spirit is saying to the churches" (Revelation 2:7a NRSV). The verse does not read, "Let anyone who has an ear listen to what the Spirit is saying to him or her." The concern in each case is not what the Spirit wants to communicate to the individual, but what the Spirit wants to communicate to the churches. We are called to consider the church as a group, and to listen to what the Spirit is saying to the whole community.

What is the spirit of the Risen Christ saying to your church? I can imagine pastors discussing this question in a Bible study or a prayer group or with the governing body of the church. It would be a way of encouraging a more expansive spirituality in the church, one that is based not on the individual but on the congregation. Such conversations could provide the preacher with substantial sermonic material for interpreting how the Spirit is calling your particular body of believers to minister here and now.

Soil, Animals, and Human Beings

Year B, Thanksgiving: Joel 2:21-27

Why is giving thanks to God so hard for human beings? In Joel even the elements and animals have good reason to thank God:

Don't fear, fertile land;
　rejoice and be glad,
　　for the LORD is
　　　about to do great things!
Don't be afraid, animals of the field,
　for the meadows of the wilderness will turn green;
　the tree will bear its fruit;
　　the fig tree and grapevine will give their full yield. (Joel 2:21-22)

Why is it that we are quick to let God know our need, and reticent to offer gratitude? I think what is involved in learning to thank God is the same pattern we observe in children learning to say "thanks." They do not do it automatically. We have to teach them. How many times were you told as a child, "Say 'thank you' "? How many times, if you are a parent, have you reminded your children: "Say 'thank you' "? However, when we become adults, I believe it takes something more sophisticated than such early childhood instructions. Becoming an adult involves mastering so many complex tasks that we develop a sense of autonomy and self-achievement, which can block our awareness of how totally dependent we are upon the source of every good and perfect gift. Therefore, our preaching needs to foster the recovery of gratitude by breaking through the illusion of self-sufficiency. That is exactly what Joel does by placing his exhortation to the "Children of Zion" (Joel 2:23) in the context of speaking to the soil and the animals. He reminds us that instead of being autonomous we are utterly dependent upon natural processes that are in turn utterly dependent upon God.

Picture yourself in the kitchen preparing the Thanksgiving meal. You have all the food and ingredients spread out on the counter: vegetables, seasonings, nuts, flour, cranberries, turkey. But this day before you begin you read aloud from Joel:

> Children of Zion,
>> rejoice and be glad
>>> in the LORD your God;
>> because he will give you the early rain. . . .
> The threshing floors will be full of grain;
>> the vats will overflow with new wine and fresh oil. (Joel 2:23-24)

Say, "Thank you!"

The Possibility of Obeying Impossible Commandments

Year B, Thanksgiving: Matthew 6:25-33

If we were to isolate the commandments that Christ gives in the Sermon on the Mount, and print them all up as maxims for daily living to stick on our walls or on our kitchen bulletin board, it would be blatantly obvious that there is no way we human beings can live up to what Christ preaches: "Give to those who ask, and don't refuse those who wish to borrow from you" (Matthew 5:42). We have enough worldly wisdom to know that if we obey this command we will be begged and borrowed into poverty. "Love your enemies and pray for those who harass you" (Matthew 5:44). We have enough hard-earned realism to know if we obey this command our enemies will crush us. "Don't worry about your life, what you'll eat or what you'll drink, or about your body" (Matthew 6:25). We have enough self-knowledge to realize that we cannot command worries to disappear.

There is no hope we will live out Christ's commandments, no hope at all, unless—unless there is some radically different way of perceiving and understanding life. And that is what Christ gives us when he invites us to consider the lilies that "neither toil nor spin, yet I tell you, even Solomon in all his glory was not clothed like one of these" (Matthew 6:28b-29 NRSV). Christ is not romanticizing nature. Instead, he is pointing to the processes of creation that function independently of our worldly wisdom and that produce astonishing beauty. It is a beauty that has the capacity, if we would only look with receptive eyes and hearts, to startle us into a state of wonder and faith.

The commandments, then, are not isolated moral exhortations. They are the fruit of grounding ourselves in the one who is the source of the lilies' splendor, and by extension, the source of all the glories about us that we did nothing to create: trees and rivers, seas and mountains, planets and stars. When we realize that existence itself is an act of grace, we then receive the grace that makes it possible to live the impossible commandments that Christ gives us.

CHAPTER 4

YEAR C

An Unmet Hunger, Simple to Meet

Year C, Advent 1: 1 Thessalonians 3:9-13, Advent 2: Philippians 1:3-11

Several years ago I was in a small airport far away from home, washing my hands in the men's room. It was the most immaculate public restroom I had ever used. Everything shone. The floors looked as clean as hospital floors. Out of the corner of my eye I caught sight of the janitor polishing one of the mirrors. I could see how he eyed his work to make sure it was perfect. When we came face-to-face, I spontaneously blurted out, "Thank you so much for the way you clean this place. I have never seen such a clean restroom."

With equal impetuosity, the man looked at me with tears springing to his eyes and said, "Thank you for noticing. No one has ever thanked me in all the years I have worked here."

I do not know what possessed me to speak to the man. It was just one of those promptings that leapt out of me. What I have never forgotten about that brief exchange are the tears in the man's eyes and the mixture of sadness and gratitude in his voice: sadness for all the years of never being acknowledged, gratitude for a brief encounter with another human being who appreciated his work. It gave me a profound glimpse into the human heart: we yearn and hunger to have someone recognize and celebrate the value of what we do and are.

With deep feeling, the Apostle Paul speaks to this yearning and hunger. He asks the Thessalonians, "How can we thank God enough for you, given all the joy we have because of you before our God?" (1 Thessalonians 3:9). He declares in Philippians 1:3-5: "I thank my God every time I mention you in my prayers. I'm thankful for all of you every time I pray, and it's always a prayer full of joy. I'm glad because of the way you have been my partners in the ministry of the gospel from the time you first believed it until now."

Do you ever start a sermon with such affirmation of your congregation? There are people sitting there whose faithful ministry has never had the holy praise it deserves. Imagine what it would mean to hear such a word from you.

Why Preaching Matters

Year C, Advent 2: Luke 3:1-6, Advent 4: Luke 1:39-45

I recall a conversation with a gifted Doctor of Ministry student, a fine preacher and pastor, a minister who gives me hope for the church and the world because of her eloquence on behalf of the gospel and because her whole manner of being and doing matches the truth of Christ that she proclaims.

She came to talk with me about why preaching matters. For her there is no doubt about the importance of preaching. She told me how her own life was "utterly transformed by a particular sermon that I heard at just the time I needed to hear it." But she had met many preachers who wondered if preaching does matter, especially amidst the splash and glitz of the media and the overwhelming supply of information and misinformation on the Web. Preachers work to craft what they say, but they are haunted by a suspicion that often subverts their homiletical energies: what difference can their meager words make when the world is consumed with power brokers and superstars?

The issue is as ancient as the gospel. If two thousand years ago in Palestine you had asked the man or woman on the street who the movers and shakers were, he or she would probably have named the same big guns that Luke does: Emperor Tiberius, Pontius Pilate, Herod, Philip, Lysanias, and Caiaphas (Luke 3:1-2). Those are the figures that would be featured on the covers of *Time* and *People*. They are the ones who would be interviewed on the morning news. A young woman finding herself pregnant going to visit a companionable older woman for three months (Luke 1:39-44) would not even make the back page.

What did it matter that some poor woman was going to have a child? Amidst the glitz and splash of imperial Roman power, it was nothing. Nothing at all. But you and I know now that what appeared to matter most then has long been forgotten, and what appeared inconsequential then was in fact the greatest news of all. Faithful preaching recapitulates the pattern of Christ's birth: something small and insignificant in the world's eyes is in truth the power of God flowing into the human community. That is why preaching matters.

Clear Out the Cluttered Heart

Year C, Advent 3: Luke 3:7-18, Advent 4: Luke 1:39-45

The amount of clutter I accumulate in my in-box and office is exceeded only by the amount of clutter I accumulate in my heart. But I am not alone in this. Worries, regrets, and doubts can fill any human heart to overflowing. What does it take to clear the mess out?

By the end of the school year my office reaches a state of clutter *maximus*, yet since the students have left for the summer and no one is around, I let it sit there. But as fall approaches, I know students and colleagues will be coming back, and prompted by the expectation of their e-mail inquiries and their knocking at the door, I move into action. I clean out my in-box, throw out papers I no longer need, get things filed away, return books to the library, and get ready to receive my visitors.

The same pattern holds for the heart. If I am going to extend hospitality and be truly attentive, I need to clear out all the stuff that will leave no room for my guests' words and needs to find a welcome place in my heart.

Advent is the season to clear out the cluttered heart. Isaac Watts said it perfectly when he wrote: "Let every heart prepare [Christ] room." Two of our Gospel readings for this month demonstrate ways to prepare room. One is Elizabeth's response to Mary's visit. Instead of focusing on her own health and welfare, a perfectly understandable human response given that she is pregnant so late in life, Elizabeth lays aside all self-preoccupation to welcome with joyful hospitality her kinswoman and the Christ whom she is bearing in her body (Luke 1:42-45).

The second way to prepare the heart is shown in John's answer to the crowds who asked him, "What then should we do?" (Luke 3:10). John's pointed commands effectively add up to two basic actions: show compassion and live with integrity (Luke 3:10-14). If we follow the pattern of Elizabeth and John, we will clear out our cluttered hearts and have ample room for the one who is coming to take up residence within us and among us.

Testifying Against Apparent Truth

Years A, B, and C, Christmas Day: John 1:1-14

It may be that I have watched too many legal dramas on television and at the movies. But one of the staples of such entertainment—from *Perry Mason* to *Law and Order* to *My Cousin Vinny*—is the scene in which a witness must give testimony that at first appears absurd to the jury. The prosecutor usually jumps all over the defense: "Out of order. That's absurd, Your Honor." But then the defense attorney or the witness makes a plea to the bench and the objection is overruled. The witness sticks to his or her original claim, and eventually everyone comes to see the truth of the testimony. If the witness wavered or hesitated for a moment, the game would be over. The case hangs on the steadfastness and accuracy of the witness in the face of initial appearances that overwhelmingly suggest that the truth is exactly the opposite of what the witness claims.

"[John] came as a witness to testify concerning the light, so that through him everyone would believe in the light" (John 1:7). There were people ready to jump all over John the Baptist for his testimony to the light of Christ: "Who are you? We need to give an answer to those who sent us. What do you say about yourself?" (John 1:22). But John did not waver. He was crystal clear and utterly steadfast about his testimony. He had come to testify to the light, and he did not back down even though the state of the world appeared to contradict his claim, even though the thick gloom of human conflict and brokenness seemed to discredit his witness.

There are all kinds of sentimental and emotional reasons why people look forward to this season of the year. But perhaps these reasons do not fully account for why people celebrate Christmas. Perhaps there is a more profound reality interwoven with all of their yearnings and expectations: somewhere in their hearts they know that the witness John gives to the light is the ultimate truth about life. They come once again to hear the reliable testimony, the testimony that against all appearances is forever true: "The light shines in the darkness, / and the darkness doesn't extinguish the light" (John 1:5).

The Connective Tissue of the Spirit

Year C, Epiphany 1: Luke 3:15-17, 21-22, Epiphany 3: 1 Corinthians 12:12-31a

If you have ever whacked your thumb with a hammer or burned your hand, you know how your whole body seems to be concentrated in that one injured part. People talk with you, but you find your listening abilities constricted by the pain. When the wound finally heals, it is as though the whole body were made new, and your capacity to listen and to comprehend returns.

Paul the apostle uses this phenomenon to explain what happens to the body of Christ when any one member is hurt or healed: "If one member suffers, all suffer together with it; if one member is honored, all rejoice together with it" (1 Corinthians 12:26 NRSV). Paul is talking in idealistic terms about how the body of Christ responds to the suffering of its members. We know from the rest of the apostle's correspondence that the Corinthians did not in fact live up to the high ideal he proclaimed. They were busy asserting their own spiritual superiority or exercising their class bias when they gathered.

Nevertheless, Paul's statement of the ideal awakens a powerful hope in us. I think of times when I have seen churches respond to a suffering member as if they were indeed connected by a tissue of Spirit that made them one body. If you have ever observed this or experienced it yourself, then you know that this is a pattern of being and doing that helps make human suffering bearable and amplifies human joy. How can we encourage this deep empathic behavior?

One way is to meditate upon and pray our way into the baptism of Jesus. Christ does not stand aloof from the need for repentance and renewal, but rather identifies with the human condition by joining with others in baptism (Luke 3:21). Through this action Christ reveals what it means to be one with the human family in its brokenness and in its transformation. When we as the body of Christ suffer with each other and rejoice with each other, then we are continuing in our corporate life the very action that awakens from the heart of God this gracious affirmation: "With you I am well pleased" (Luke 3:22 NRSV).

Lifetime Ambiguities of Ministry

Year C, Epiphany 1: Luke 3:15-17, 21-22, Epiphany 2: John 2:1-11,
Epiphany 3: Luke 4:14-21, Epiphany 4: Luke 4:21-30

What are your first memories of being a minister or priest or lay leader in the church? Are your memories relatively recent or do they stretch back over many years? My hunch is that no matter how long ago your ministry began, you can conjure up the excitement and the anxiety, the pride and the embarrassment, that attended some of your first acts as a pastor, chaplain, or church leader.

The first Sundays of Epiphany are filled with memories of Jesus' early ministry. Although they are not exact parallels to our own experience, the accounts resonate with realities we have known. The scenes are a mixture of boldness and enthusiasm, perplexity and resistance—the very qualities that most of us can recall as we started out.

There is the intense presence of the Spirit (Luke 3:22), the wonder of holy things miraculously happening (John 2:11), the praise of those who are touched by the freshness of a new ministry (Luke 4:15), and the pride of one's home community of faith (Luke 4:22). As we recall these moments in Jesus' life and their echoes in our own experience, our hearts may fill with more than nostalgia. We may feel again the warm affection and high hopes that energized us as we began to minister.

Yet in the midst of these affirmations, Christ encounters the powers with whom he will tangle for the rest of his ministry. There is the strong hand of the Roman government that arrests John the Baptist (Luke 3:18-20) and that will come for Jesus later on. There is the home congregation that initially delights in his ministry, then drives him out of town to throw him over a cliff when he preaches the all-inclusive grace of God (Luke 4:23-29). This fickle behavior will emerge again in the mob that greets Jesus on Palm Sunday and calls for his crucifixion on Good Friday.

I cannot help but wonder if Jesus were tempted to ask, why did I ever begin this ministry in the first place? We believe Jesus to be fully human—and part of being fully human is to question if we are doing the right thing when we run into opposition and the resistance of a hostile world. Seeing what happened to John the Baptist, with his own heart pounding as he walked away from the angry mob on the crest of the hill, Jesus might have been tempted to tone down his message. He might have yearned for the unambiguous success of his first efforts: "He . . . was praised by everyone" (Luke 4:15) and "everyone was raving about Jesus" (Luke 4:22). Instead, "he passed through the crowd and went on his way" (Luke 4:30), carrying the ambiguities of ministry all the way to the cross.

Biblical Ambiguity as a Form of Revelation

Year C, Epiphany 2: Isaiah 62:1-5

Sometimes in consulting commentaries I discover interpretations that are at odds with one another. I often choose one interpretation over the other to guide my preparation and creation of the sermon. But there are times when, instead of resolving the ambiguity, I use it as a way of opening myself to deeper theological meaning. Isaiah 62:1-5 is a casebook example. I read it and ask: who is speaking these words? My study Bible assures me that it is the prophet, but reading the text closely, I am not convinced. It might be the prophet, but it also sounds as though it might be God. So I turn to a commentary and read, "It is difficult to determine who sings this song."[1] Perhaps it is God who is finally breaking heaven's self-acknowledged silence:

> I've kept still for a very long time.
> I've been silent
> and restrained myself.
> Like a woman in labor I will moan;
> I will pant, I will gasp. (Isaiah 42:14)

I turn to another commentary that claims it is the prophet speaking but acknowledges others have thought it to be Yahweh. The scholars leave me with the same ambiguity that drove me to consult them in the first place!

I reflect on what the ambiguity might mean. Perhaps both schools of interpretation are right. Perhaps the prophet is speaking, and through the prophet's speaking we overhear the heart of God speaking. In other words, the ambiguity is a human-divine ambiguity that expresses the complexity of human speech to, for, and about God. The prophet pledges to keep reminding God to restore Zion and vindicate the city before the eyes of the whole world. But the intensity of the prophet's commitment represents the very intensity that characterizes the will of God, who cares passionately about Jerusalem and its people. Through the prophet's speech we hear the stirrings within God's own heart. The ambiguity of who speaks is a revelation about the nature of revelation: God is sometimes known through human speech addressed to God. Listen to what you say to God that flows from the deepest yearnings of the human heart and you may hear God speaking.

Religious Spirituality and Spiritual Religion

Year C, Epiphany 3: Luke 4:14-21

S*pirituality, spiritual formation, spiritual direction,* and *the spiritual life:* I have heard and read these words repeatedly in recent years, and not just in religious circles. There is even a sociological category that I encountered in a serious scholarly proposal: "spiritual but not religious," a designation so frequently used by those investigating the phenomenon that they have reduced the phrase to an acronym: SBNR! (People who claim such an identity are SBNRs.) I am not a sociologist of religion or an expert on this topic, but I have read enough articles to gain the impression that, from the perspective of many SBNRs, *religion* is oppressive because it is about structures, institutions, beliefs, and rules, whereas *spirituality* is enlivening because it puts us in touch with the vital essence of mystery, wonder, and beauty.

The bifurcation of religion and spirituality is utterly missing from the way Luke presents Christ. Instead, religion and spirituality are interfused realities so that we can no more separate one from the other than we can separate the cream from the coffee once we have mixed them together in our cup. There is a striking incidence of this in Luke 4. No sooner is Jesus described as "filled with the power of the Spirit" (Luke 4:14 NRSV) than we also learn that it was his "custom" to attend synagogue on the Sabbath (Luke 4:16 NRSV). Furthermore, Jesus clearly had learned the traditions of his faith, because when he is handed the scroll of the prophet Isaiah, he knows how to unroll it and find the verses he wants to read.

Jesus is a rabbi who participates in the religious practices of his community. He understands its structures, institutions, beliefs, and rules. But instead of oppressing him, these practices provide openings into the liberating work of God. In his sermon he draws upon the community's tradition in order to present how God often works through those outside the community. His reading of the tradition angers the hometown crowd, but it is alive with the mystery, wonder, and beauty of God's grace and spirit. Jesus achieves a vital spirituality not by abandoning religion, but by employing its practices to draw us into the liberating presence of the living Spirit. Christ gives us a religious spirituality and a spiritual religion, inseparably interfused.

Pastoring the Church of Corinth

Year C, Epiphany 4: 1 Corinthians 13:1-13, Epiphany 5: Luke 5:1-11,
Epiphany 6: Luke 6:17-26, Lent 1: Deuteronomy 26:1-11

The trustee meeting is a minefield, and somebody manages to step on every mine in the room. The Nurture and Care Committee ends its meeting in a volley of fierce exchanges between two factions. The administrative assistant reports a number of angry phone calls about a decision you made that you thought was a done deal.

You go into your office to collect your thoughts for Sunday's sermon. To get things out of your system you let your mind float among the many scriptural passages you have been studying for Epiphany and Lent. You recall the command to "celebrate all the good things the LORD your God has done for you and your family" (Deuteronomy 26:11), and you grumble about the bounty of minefields among the trustees. You hear the distant echo of Christ saying, "Row out farther, into the deep water, and drop your nets for a catch" (Luke 5:4), and you imagine commanding the Nurture and Care Committee to set out into the deep water of great human need that calls for their attention. You consider the angry phone calls, and Christ's voice returns to you yet again, "How terrible for you when all speak well of you. / Their ancestors did the same things to the false prophets" (Luke 6:26). Trusting that Christ can handle it, you emit a bitter retort: "Yes, but it feels like hell when they *don't* speak well of you."

You walk to the office window and look out. You say to yourself, "How can I preach to this ornery, conflicted community?" You open the window to get some fresh air. You read the familiar sign on the church's front lawn: "The Church of Paul the Apostle in Corinth." A wind blows through the window and you rush to your desk and begin typing rapidly. The words almost make your heart stop because you know they did not come from your tangled soul: "If I speak in tongues of human beings and of angels but I don't have love, I'm a clanging gong or a clashing cymbal. . . . Love is patient. . . . Love puts up with all things, trusts in all things, hopes for all things, endures all things" (1 Corinthians 13:1-7).

A Connection More Essential Than Being Online

Year C, Epiphany 5: 1 Corinthians 15:1-11, Epiphany 6: Jeremiah 17:5-10,
Epiphany 7: Luke 6:27-38, Transfiguration: Exodus 34:29-35

Consider two plants: "a shrub in the desert" and "a tree planted by water." The contrast is a primal metaphor about different ways of being: parched and shriveled or green and fruitful. Jeremiah offers us these images as part of a Wisdom poem (Jeremiah 17:5-10 NRSV). They present an essential choice that lies before ancient Israel, a nation that has failed to live up to its social-ethical responsibility.

What kind of plant are we? Whether we are a tree or a shrub depends on what we are rooted in. The shrub ekes out existence "in the parched places of the wilderness, in an uninhabited salt land," while the tree thrives, "sending out its roots by the stream" (Jeremiah 17:6, 8 NRSV). Even though the prophet didn't foresee or intend this, his metaphorical contrast provides an image for holding together several of the lections for Epiphany and Transfiguration Sunday. Each lection deals with what happens when we are deeply rooted in God or when that connection is disrupted.

Moses had such deep roots in the divine presence that it was apparent to anyone who saw him—although he was not immediately aware of the transformation because it was not something he achieved himself but that was bestowed upon him by God: "Moses didn't realize that the skin of his face shone brightly because he had been talking with God" (Exodus 34:29). The change in Moses' countenance represented the fruit of being rooted in God. Moses was a tree, not a shrub.

Those who give with wild extravagance to meet the needs of others are also trees bearing fruit. Their generosity flows from the nature of God, for they are living the instruction of Jesus: "Be compassionate just as your Father[/Mother] is compassionate" (Luke 6:36).

A tree can turn into a shrub. We might be rooted near living water for a while during our lives, but then a change of circumstance or commitment can transplant us from a fertile environment to "an uninhabited salt land." This appears to be what happened to the community of Corinth. Paul reminds them of "the good news that I preached to you," and he recites the roll of witnesses to the resurrection of Christ (1 Corinthians 15:1-8). The Corinthians had been trees, but now they were becoming shrubs whose roots were no longer reaching into the rich soil of the Risen Christ.

The final archaeological picture in Othmar Keel's *The Symbolism of the Biblical World* features a figure prostrate in prayer, beneath whom run waves of water.[2] Reaching down through the water and up through the praying figure into the heavens is an extravagantly leafy, fruited tree. That ancient figure has established a connection more essential than being online. That ancient figure, rooted in the living God, has become a tree.

Living the Prayers We Pray

Year C, Lent 1: Luke 4:1-13, Psalm 91:1-2, 9-16

How does prayer, particularly the repeated prayers of the community of faith, shape us over time? The Gospels picture Jesus as someone who called upon such prayer in his time of greatest need. In Matthew 27:46 and Mark 15:33, Jesus prays Psalm 22:1 as his final words, while in Luke 23:46 he dies after praying Psalm 31:5. Whichever it might actually have been does not matter nearly so much as the clear implication that Jesus was steeped in the Psalms, in the prayers of the community of faith. Jesus shows himself throughout the Gospels to be thoroughly grounded in the traditions of the Jewish people, including regular attendance at synagogue.

I can imagine during Lent a series of sermons on living the prayers we pray, just as Jesus lived the prayers he prayed. Consider, for example, when Jesus responds to Satan in the wilderness. Satan tries to get Jesus to throw himself down from the pinnacle of the temple by quoting out-of-context words from Psalm 91: " 'He will command his angels concerning you, to protect you, and they will take you up in their hands so that you won't hit your foot on a stone.' " Jesus answers back, "It's been said, 'Don't test the Lord your God' " (Luke 4:10-12).

Although Jesus' response is a quotation from Deuteronomy, his stand against Satan's temptation flows naturally from the psalm verse that Satan omits when he tempts Jesus: "You'll march on top of lions and vipers; / you'll trample young lions and serpents underfoot" (Psalm 91:13). No wonder Satan does not quote this verse! It affirms that the faithful person will overcome the destructive forces that Satan personifies. Jesus is so filled with the fullness of the psalmist's prayer that he is able to withstand the misuse of the psalm to tempt him.

Explore Christ's journey to the cross and resurrection in light of the whole of Psalm 91, or any other number of psalms. The Lenten pilgrimage can become a way of seeing in Christ what it means to live the prayers we pray.

A Deep and Terrifying Darkness

Year C, Lent 2: Genesis 15:1-12, 17-18

We usually associate a revelation from God with light. Truth or wisdom or an essential message shines clearly before us. But among our readings this month is a very different manifestation of revelation.

God has promised Abram that his children will be as numberless as the stars. Abram believes the promise, and "the LORD reckoned it to him as righteousness" (Genesis 15:6 NRSV). God then gives Abram directions for an act of ritual sacrifice. But no sooner is the sacrifice prepared than we read, "As the sun was going down, a deep sleep fell upon Abram, and a deep and terrifying darkness descended upon him" (Genesis 15:12 NRSV). The subsequent revelation from God includes a prediction from God of the Hebrews' enslavement in Egypt. What a striking contrast there is between the revelation that Abram's children will be as the stars of night, and the "deep and terrifying darkness" that brings with it the knowledge of enslavement in Egypt.

Textual critics see verses 13-16 as an insertion by some editor, and indeed this does seem to make sense because verses 17-18 are clearly a continuation of the earlier story. But whether the textual critics are right or not, the way the text stands, the way it blends promise and hope with "a deep and terrifying darkness," is worthy of reflection by all of us who preach. Without the deep and terrifying darkness, the promise of the future becomes too facile. We are left only with the loveliness of the twinkling stars as a sign of a future. But with the deep and terrifying darkness the promise takes on realism it would otherwise lack: Abram's children will multiply, but his descendants will face a hard and cruel world.

The deep and terrifying darkness provides a richer understanding of revelation: yes, revelation makes known the bright and shining promise of God, but revelation also discloses the brutality of human beings. Therefore, if our sermons are to be faithful to the revelation of God, we must be open not only to the promise, but also to the deep and terrifying darkness that engages us with the hard truth of humanity's inhumanity.

Lent as a Season of Suffering and Hope

Year C, Lent 2: Psalm 27

I attend an exhibition of war photographs. They were taken by a number of professional photographers. I look and weep. The wounded stare out at us with haunted eyes; the dead lie in the streets in pools of blood; smoke and flame rise from bombed out vehicles. The suffering is so great that at times I have to turn away to gain strength to look at the next photograph.

I return from the photographs to my office and sit down to read the upcoming lectionary readings for Lent. The first thing I read is Psalm 27. I stop cold at the third verse:

> If an army camps against me,
>   my heart won't be afraid.
> If war comes up against me,
>   I will continue to trust.

The remembered images of the photographs sweep upon me, and I speak the words of the verse aloud into the air of my office, trying to hold back the horror. Can I really pray as the psalmist prays and mean it?

I read the next verse of the psalm:

> I have asked one thing
> from the LORD—
> it's all I seek—
>   to live in the LORD's house
>   all the days of my life,
>   seeing the LORD's beauty
>   and constantly adoring his temple. (Psalm 27:4)

The psalmist's hope only makes the unspeakable sorrow of the photographs deeper and sharper.

To read these two verses side by side in the midst of Lent and in the face of the terror of war is to make our way toward Christ's passion and death with a heart filled with suffering and hope, with the burden of human violence and the resilience of human yearning for "the LORD's beauty." Perhaps our sermons in Lent should simply move back and forth between what is happening in our violent world and what happens in the Bible as Christ moves toward Jerusalem and death. Yet in every sermon we will recall the irrepressible hope of the human heart for the beauty of God. How is Christ leading us through the suffering and from the suffering to the realization of that magnificent, holy hope?

Grumbling and the Flutter of Holy Wings

Year C, Lent 2: Luke 13:31-35, Lent 4: Luke 15:1-3, 11b-32

There is a whole lot of grumbling going on in these Lenten readings. The good religious folk are grumbling about Jesus' hospitality to the riffraff of society (Luke 15:2). The older brother in one of

Jesus' best-known parables is grumbling that Dad never gave him a big party even though he has been a faithful worker and son year after year (Luke 15:28-30). And as for the city of Jerusalem, it does more than grumble; it is "the city that kills the prophets and stones those who are sent to it" (Luke 13:34 NRSV).

If I picked up the Bible not knowing what the book was and fingered through its pages perusing these particular passages, I might well decide: who needs this? It is all about malcontents and grumblers and murderers. I might put the Bible down and search the shelves for something more inspiring, more positive and uplifting. I might look for something reassuring like a self-help book or perhaps a magazine that entices me with photographs of the rich and famous gathered in their sumptuous homes.

The Bible is a terrible book for feeding such fantasies. Why then does it exert an enduring hold upon the human imagination? Because, I believe, there is deep within us a knowledge that we try to hide from ourselves but that we can never permanently suppress: the knowledge that we *are* grumblers, always fighting for our own faction and discounting any others. It is the knowledge that we are the good religious folk, incensed when someone who ought to know better welcomes riffraff to the same party to which we have been invited. It is the knowledge that we are the older brother or sister, furious with resentment at the grace that Mom and Dad have shown to our undeserving sibling. It is the knowledge that we are citizens of a society as violent as Jerusalem, "the city that kills the prophets."

The Bible empowers us to come to terms with the devastating truth about our humanity by supplying us with visions of the God whose grace and grandeur are expansive enough to transform our malcontent, grumbling, violent lives. Are we grumbling Corinthians? We are baptized into Christ! Are we angry older siblings? Our parent insists, "Everything that I have is yours" (Luke 15:31). Are we citizens in a violent society? Christ would gather us as a hen gathers her brood (Luke 13:34). We can face the reality of our humanity because of a greater reality: the grace of God. Listen with the heart of faith, and from the core and source of life you will hear not grumbling, but the flutter of holy wings.

With What Set of Ears Are We Listening to Jesus?

Year C, Lent 4: Luke 15:1-3, 11b-32

It was an astounding range of listeners who first heard the parable of the spendthrift child, the responsible older brother, and the father of extravagant love. Luke 15:3 introduces the story by saying, "Jesus told them this parable." If *them* refers to all the parties listed in verses 1-2, then the crowd included tax collectors, sinners, Pharisees, and scribes. We might take the word *them* to refer only to the Pharisees and scribes, but that reading strikes me as too constricted, since the first verse describes the tax collectors and scribes as "gathering around Jesus to listen." I assume that *them* refers to the whole lot, the prim and the proper, the outcasts and the inner circle, sinners and good religious folk, all listening together. It must have been tense given that one party was "grumbling" against the other (Luke 15:2).

Those varied listeners surely heard Jesus' parable with different ears. One way to awaken a fresh hearing of Jesus' now well-worn words is to invite listeners to hear the story from two different perspectives. By imagining the varied reactions of Jesus' first listeners, they may free themselves to hear the story anew. First, invite them to listen as people who are considered outsiders, losers, failures, the dregs of society. Or maybe, depending on your congregation, they were prodigal investors who blew their money on stock funds that promised returns so exaggerated that they were beyond realistic expectation. Once the congregation members have settled into their roles, read the parable without interruption.

Then have them imagine themselves as Pharisees and scribes. It is essential that you not present these folks as bad people. They are in fact good, responsible, successful, reliable, capable, and hard working. Once your listeners have settled into these new roles, read the parable again without interruption.

Then in the rest of the sermon wonder aloud what actions and thoughts stood out for them, first as tax collectors and sinners, then as Pharisees and scribes. Next reflect on how we hear things differently based on who we are and what we bring to the act of listening. Finally, you can conclude with a simple question: with what set of ears are we listening to Jesus?

Seeing What Is Out of Sight

Year C, Palm/Passion Sunday: Luke 23:1-49

The more something is hidden, the more we want to see it.
I picture people stopping to look through the peep holes that
contractors often provide for "sidewalk superintendents." The
onlookers might be wondering, how deep is the foundation? Or I think of
paintings I have seen where a figure in full view is looking off beyond the
border of the canvas toward someone else whose arm or shoulder is all
that is shown to us. What does that hidden person look like?

What we see draws us to consider what we do not see. I believe our
ancient forebears understood this at a profound level. In the way they
pictured the relationship between what we know of the divine and what
is hidden in mystery, they expressed the human desire to see reality
more completely.

The holy of holies in the temple was a symbolic representation of
both God's revelation and God's hiddenness. In the first chapter of
Luke, Zechariah the priest is chosen by lot to enter the sanctuary.
There he encounters an angel of the Lord, who tells Zechariah that his
wife, Elizabeth, will bear John the Baptist. Zechariah is granted a revelation in the sanctuary, in the place hidden from the view of others. The people outside "wondered at his delay in the sanctuary," and
understood from his silence that "he had seen a vision in the sanctuary" (Luke 1:21-22 NRSV).

It is instructive to remember this scene when we turn to Luke's account
of the crucifixion in which he writes: "The sun stopped shining. Then the
curtain in the sanctuary tore down the middle" (Luke 23:45). Whereas
Luke's Gospel begins by alternating between the revealed and the hidden,
Luke's account of the crucifixion suggests that through the death of Jesus
we are granted a view into the very heart of the divine. The torn curtain
represents a breakthrough—the divine hiddenness giving way to a startling clarity about the character of God. What do we preachers see in that
moment of revelation? What is the nature of the God who is made
known? In our response to that question lie the purpose and passion of
our calling to proclaim the gospel.

Futile Strategies for Resisting God

Year C, Lent 5: Isaiah 43:16-21, Palm/Passion Sunday: Luke 23:1-49,
Easter Vigil: Luke 24:1-12, Easter 3: John 21:1-19,
Years A, B, and C, Easter 2: John 20:19-31

I once had a neighbor whose cellar would now and then fill with water from a source he could not locate. He tried every standard remedy to seal and stop the pesky, persistent element. Finally he hired an engineer who was a specialist in such matters. The engineer discovered that there was an underground stream that flowed directly beneath the center of my neighbor's foundation and whenever the subterranean water rose, there was nothing that could stop it. The only solution was to open the cellar and dig a trench in the floor that allowed the water to flow unimpeded.

God's work among us is very much like that persistent underground stream, and our responses are often similar to my neighbor's. We attempt to block and eradicate holy powers that we will never be able to command.

In the passages listed above, we see religious people devising futile strategies to stop or deny the redeeming work of God. There is the strategy of idolizing the past: remembering the great deeds that God once did long ago while ignoring the "new thing" that God is doing in the present (Isaiah 43:16-21). There is the mob psychology strategy of playing to people's fears about the new teacher who is "perverting the people" (Luke 23:2 NRSV), and appealing to the very worst in human nature (Luke 23:1-49). There is the strategy of discounting the witness of the outcasts, reckoning that what they have to say is nothing more than "an idle tale" (Luke 24:1-12). There is the strategy of trying to lock the doors against the threatening world and cowering in fear (John 20:19-31). And there is the strategy of retreating to what we used to do, to pretending we can simply start up where we left off before God intruded upon our life and transformed our whole way of being (John 21:1-19). That is quite a list of strategies, and there is not one of us who has not tried one or all of them at some point.

The major problem with all of these strategies is that none of them work. The stories of the exiles' return from Babylon, of Christ's resurrection, of the disciples receiving the Holy Spirit, of Christ feeding the disciples by the lake—all point to a persistent, unstoppable stream of grace and life that flows from the deep, dear core of things.

Once my neighbor gave up his futile efforts at stopping the subterranean stream and allowed it to flow through its new streambed in his cellar, the house would sometimes sing with the music of running water. Just imagine the song that would sound in our hearts and churches if we gave up our futile strategies of trying to resist the irrepressible God!

Preaching to a Primal Fear

Year C, Easter 1: 1 Corinthians 15:19-26

My teaching partner and I regularly ask the members of our introductory preaching class to write one page describing the sermon they would most like to hear preached. The exercise is based on the observation that the best sermons preachers deliver are often the ones they preach to themselves—not *about* themselves, but *to* themselves. The assignment usually engages the preachers' deepest fears and needs, their highest hopes and profoundest longings. It puts them in touch with their humanity as finite creatures shaped from the dust of the earth, and in doing so it opens them to the vulnerabilities that they share with all the rest of us.

The last time we assigned this exercise, we received a paper from a healthy young student who was about twenty-three years old and who above all other subjects was hungering for a sermon on the resurrection—not resurrection in this life, not resurrection as a paradigm for our daily way of being and doing, but the final resurrection, when as Paul puts it, there at last "comes the end, when [Christ] hands over the kingdom to God the Father, after he has destroyed every ruler and every authority and power. For he must reign until he has put all his enemies under his feet. The last enemy to be destroyed is death" (1 Corinthians 15:24-26 NRSV). The student was not arguing for pie-in-the-sky Christianity, not asking us to abandon our passion for justice and compassion in this life. Rather the student was acknowledging the primal fear of death, a fear that when left unaddressed may distort how we live as individuals and communities here and now. When we shared the student's paper in class, it was riveting.

When was the last time you preached about the resurrection? Our student speculated that our technology and the artificial environments in which we live might nurture the illusion that we are more in control of reality than in fact we are. The result is that we fail to proclaim resurrection as plainly as Paul, who reminds us: "If we have a hope in Christ only in this life, then we deserve to be pitied more than anyone else" (1 Corinthians 15:19).

Long Ago and Far Away, Here and Now, Forever

Year C, Easter 4: John 10:22-30, Easter 5: John 13:31-35, Easter 6: John 14:23-29, Easter 7: John 17:20-26

Sometimes the gospel sounds like a fairy tale—the story of a good man who lived far away and long ago. The distance in time frees the heart to play, to entertain visions of extravagant hope that the stress and strain of daily life would otherwise suppress. There is, however, a theological trap in the fairy tale version of the gospel: Christ is confined to a past that the present can never recover. The gospel beckons from the land of what once was but is no longer.

Perhaps the story of Jesus had become something of a fairy tale to members of John's community before the evangelist wrote his Gospel. Their great-grandparents had told their grandparents who had told their parents who had told them the stories about Jesus: water turned to wine, a crowd of five thousand fed with a little boy's lunch, a rigged trial, an empty grave, a meal by the lake at sunrise. By the time John wrote his Gospel, these had become stories of long ago and far away. What once were vivid memories were beginning to sound more like fables, something that would awaken the questions of every doubting Thomas.

John uses an interesting literary device to give witness to the living Christ. Although John employs regular grammatical tenses, he writes in such a way that the barriers between past, present, and future collapse. Jesus speaks directly not only to the audience in the story but to us as well. Instead of fairy tale time, the gospel of Christ is "Once upon a time long ago and far away—here and now—forever." Again and again in John's Gospel, Christ addresses simultaneously the characters in the passage, John's own church, ourselves, and generations yet unborn: "My sheep listen to my voice. I know them and they follow me" (John 10:27).

"This is how everyone will know that you are my disciples, when you love each other" (John 13:35). "Peace I leave with you. My peace I give you. I give to you not as the world gives. Don't be troubled or afraid" (John 14:27). "I pray they will be one, Father, just as you are in me and I am in you. I pray that they also will be in us, so that the world will believe that you sent me" (John 17:21). The story of Christ is no longer a stock of well-loved but distant memories from the past. What happened back then is happening here and now.

John's Gospel does what we pray all of our sermons might do, that in the act of telling the good news we will find ourselves and our congregations in the presence of Christ who is long ago and far away—here and now—forever.

Singing Hymns at Midnight

Year C, Easter 4: Revelation 7:9-17, Easter 5: Revelation 21:1-6, Easter 7: Acts 16:16-34

Trees that grow out of solid rock have long fascinated me. I often come upon them while climbing in the mountains. Sometimes it is a sizable tree with a thick crown of green branches. I gaze in wonder at this witness to the resilience of life, to the force of seed, sapling, and root driving apart the mountain's armor of stone.

The image of those persistent trees rises in my memory when I turn to the story of Paul and Silas, cast into prison after exorcising the demon from a slave girl (Acts 16:16-34). They had been stripped, beaten, and flogged, their feet placed in stocks. It would seem that the brutality of their treatment would finally silence their witness to the resilience of life in Christ, to the force of faith and hope. But instead their faith proves to be as stubborn and productive as those robust trees growing out of granite:

> Around midnight Paul and Silas were praying and singing hymns to God, and the other prisoners were listening to them. All at once there was such a violent earthquake that it shook the prison's foundations. The doors flew open and everyone's chains came loose. (Acts 16:25-26)

No matter what the authorities do, the force of faith in action turns out to be irrepressible.

The same pattern repeats itself in the Revelation to John. Though there are many theories about the book's process of compilation and interpretation, the author, like Paul and Silas, gives witness to the irrepressible hope of the gospel. In the face of Roman persecution, John breaks into hymns of praise (Revelation 7:12) and visions of a transformed creation (Revelation 21:1-6).

Paul, Silas, and John give us hope for our own despairing age. They remind us that the resilience of faith can break through this hardened world with the same stubborn persistence as those trees that crack through solid rock. Our preaching can be a singing of hymns at midnight and a rhapsody of visionary power that moves us to embody the promise of "a new heaven and a new earth" (Revelation 21:1).

Where Do Sermons Come From?

Year C, Easter 7: John 17:20-26

If you were to trace the creation of last Sunday's sermon all the way back to its beginning point, where would the journey end? Would it be in a question that has long gnawed away inside you? Would it be in one of the Scripture readings that leapt off the page into your heart? Did it arise from some great sadness or joy in the church that the whole congregation needed to grieve or to celebrate? Was it a scene from a blockbuster movie? Was it an insight from a commentary that helped you come to terms with a troubling biblical text? Was it some matter of grave injustice that demanded analysis and judgment?

Any of these, or a thousand more things, might be the starting point for a sermon. But for now I want to point out that the last sermon you preached started two thousand years ago! It started with the witness of Christ's disciples. Christ acknowledges this when he says, "I ask not only on behalf of these [the disciples gathered for the last discourse in John], but also on behalf of those who will believe in me through their word, that they may all be one" (John 17:20-21a NRSV). If it were not for the first generations of Christians passing on the gospel, we would have had no sermon to preach last Sunday. We believe in Christ through the word of our forebears. We are indebted to the first generation of Christ's followers who passed on their witness to the second generation who passed it on to the third generation who passed it on to the fourth generation . . . until it reached the generation who passed it on to us. Christ trusts that the disciples gathered around him will pass on the gospel. He does not qualify his hope by saying, "*if* they pass on the word about me." He is confident they will.

So whenever you wonder if it matters that you preach, remember how your sermon got started two thousand years ago and that Christ trusts and blesses you to keep the chain of witness unbroken for the coming generations. Christ prays for those who will believe through our word.

Truth Too Heavy to Bear

Year C, Trinity Sunday (First Sunday after Pentecost): John 16:12-15, Proper 6: Luke 7:36–8:3, Proper 7: Luke 8:26-39

I knew the boxes were heavier than I should be lifting. But there was no one else around, I needed to get them to the new office, and this was the only time I had free. So heaving and grunting, I carried them to the car. The next day, I could hardly move. My back, my entire body, had not been ready to bear that weight.

What is true of bodies is also true of hearts and minds. Christ sometimes says to us: "I still have many things to say to you, but you cannot bear them now. When the Spirit of truth comes, he will guide you into all the truth" (John 16:12-13a NRSV). The word *bear* (*bastazein* in Greek) means not simply to endure but to carry physically, to bear a heavy weight as in Acts 3:2 (NRSV): "And a man lame from birth was being carried [bastazein] in."

The image of truth heavier than we can bear illumines other lections as well. When Jesus accepts and forgives the woman who anoints his feet, the truth of God's grace is too heavy for Simon and his guests to carry in their hearts (Luke 7:39, 48). When Jesus heals the Gerasene demoniac, the truth of his healing power is too heavy for the community to bear (Luke 8:37).

Before we judge these people for their failure to bear the truth of Christ, we need to consider ourselves. We ourselves have often encountered truth that we were not yet ready to bear. If we are white and were raised in a racist society, our first reaction to civil rights may have been to dismiss the movement. If we are male and were imbued with a sense of privilege over women, our first response to feminism may have been defensiveness. Again and again in life there is truth that we are not yet ready to bear.

We are familiar with the lag between encountering truth and accepting truth in the church. We preach a truth that is new and startling to our congregations, and at first they are not ready to carry it into their lives. They do not have the strength to bear it. Then later someone acknowledges, "When you first said that, I fought you as hard as I could. But now I see what you mean, and it has made all the difference to me."

Sometimes we have to wait for the "Spirit of truth" who "will guide [us] into all the truth" (John 16:13 NRSV). Note that word *guide*. Coming to know the truth is a process. It takes time. It requires the grace of patience—with ourselves and our congregations—for the Spirit to conduct us to where at first we would not go, and to help us bear what we earlier were not capable of bearing.

How to Be Biblical When the Bible Is Inadequate

Year C, Trinity Sunday: John 16:12-15

Sooner or later it happens to all of us: the things we learned and always depended upon turn out to be inadequate for a new situation. The maxims our parents planted in our hearts, the wisdom we gained from our peers, the carefully filed notes from our formal education—all fail to illuminate some unexpected reality that perplexes our usual principles of thought and patterns of action. We ask in exasperation, "*Now* what do we do?"

Surely something like this happened to the community of John. They had rich traditions about Jesus that offered them guidance and wisdom. But the past is never able to address every new thing that the future flings before us. Not even all of Jesus' words and actions can do that. The Gospel of John pictures Jesus naming a principle to help the church deal with those realities that his teaching does not cover: "When the Spirit of truth comes, he will guide you into all the truth" (John 16:13 NRSV). This principle had pastoral consequences for the community of John. It suggests that their worship life must have included supplications for the illumination of the Spirit. Baffled by what Christ had never mentioned, they faithfully turned to the Spirit for help.

The verse from John has implications for us who preach now. It raises the issue of how our preaching—not just any one sermon, but our preaching over time—uses the Bible. Does our preaching give the impression that everything people need to know is in the book? Or does our preaching demonstrate how the Bible is a witness to the living spirit of God that "will guide you into all the truth"? The difference between these two has consequences for the church and its response to new knowledge and new social realities.

To recognize the inadequacy of the Bible for dealing with every new human situation is not heresy. It is instead an expression of faith in the Spirit to whom the Bible gives witness in such varied and powerful ways. Authentic biblical preaching, therefore, reaches beyond the Bible toward the new truth that keeps breaking upon us.

The Fear of Healing

Year C, Proper 7: Luke 8:26-39

You would think after the healing of someone in terrible distress that all who saw it would rejoice and give thanks. I recall such events in the life of parishes where I have both pastored and been in the pew: people whose medical procedures had restored them beyond their wildest hopes, folks rescued from the edge of the grave. In every case there were prayers of thanksgiving, prayers of overflowing gratitude, prayers of irrepressible gladness and joy. But when the demoniac in Luke 8 was healed, we read that all those who knew of his restoration, "asked Jesus to leave them; for they were seized with great fear" (Luke 8:37 NRSV). The phrase *seized with great fear* echoes how the demon had "many times . . . seized" the man (Luke 8:29 NRSV). It suggests that a power as great as the demon now possessed the community. How are we to understand the fear of healing? How are we to understand the fear that entered the supposedly sane people when the demon left its victim?

The answer lies in the measures the community had taken to isolate and suppress the demoniac: "He would be bound with leg irons and chains and placed under guard" (Luke 8:29). The man was obviously someone whose powers were such a threat to the community's equilibrium that they did whatever they could to block his disruptive force. Yet their measures had never proven adequate because "he would break his restraints, and the demon would force him into the wilderness" (Luke 8:29). Therefore, to encounter in Jesus someone who had the authority to overcome what all of their efforts had failed to do was to come face-to-face with a gift for healing that challenged their ineffectual strategies. They were "seized with great fear" because Jesus' restoration of the demoniac meant they must come to terms with the inadequacy of their own responses. They would have to give up their strategies of brute force and replace them with the grace of Christ. No wonder then that sermons filled with the healing power of Christ may awaken resistance, may leave our listeners "seized with great fear."

Instead of Fire from Heaven, Grace

Year C, Proper 8: Luke 9:51-62, Proper 10: Luke 10:25-37

Every one of us knows this dangerous story line: two religious groups are in utter disagreement. They worship in different locations, read the tradition in different ways, consider their own group the true believers while the others are heretics, and they hold to stereotypes that do not recognize a single positive trait in the other. It is an exhausting, destructive situation that surfaces again and again in the history of religion.

Luke describes its effect in one sharp detail about Jesus' journey to Jerusalem: "Along the way, they entered a Samaritan village to prepare for his arrival, but the Samaritan villagers refused to welcome him because he was determined to go to Jerusalem" (Luke 9:52b-53). The Samaritans' inhospitable response to Jesus represents generations of enmity with the Judeans. The Samaritans had long considered the shrine of Mount Gerizim rather than Zion to be the holy dwelling of God. The failure to welcome Jesus infuriates the disciples, who in return ask: "Lord, do you want us to call fire down from heaven to consume them?" (Luke 9:54b). Jesus rebukes them. But you can imagine the muttering among the disciples as they move on to another village: "Those infidels!" "Can anything good come out of Samaria? Of course not!"

In the next chapter, in front of those same disciples, Jesus tells the story of the good Samaritan (Luke 10:25-37). The good Samaritan? It must have astonished the disciples as much as it did the lawyer with whom he was talking. Jesus knows the disciples had wanted to call down fire on the Samaritans. The whole incident had only reinforced Judean stereotypes of Samaritans. So Jesus offers a story that portrays grace and compassion working through a Samaritan. By making the foreigner the hero of the parable, Jesus himself becomes a good Samaritan: he sees the human community wounded and half dead because of vicious intolerance for one another. He tends to the wound by attesting to the best possible qualities of those who rejected him. The parable is not just about individual acts of compassion, but about healing the larger social divisions that threaten to destroy us.

The Problem with a Religion of Right Answers

Year C, Proper 8: Galatians 5:1, 13-25, Proper 10: Luke 10:25-37, Proper 12: Luke 11:1-13

Right answers. Our earliest schooling rewards us for them: right answers bring the teacher's approval and praise. Right answers bring good report cards. Right answers gain us admission to the college of our choice. Right answers win promotion and the boss's approval.

"You have answered correctly," Jesus says to the lawyer who has affirmed that love of God and love of neighbor are the way to eternal life (Luke 10:28). The man graduates *cum laude* in religious studies! Now that he has the degree the difficult part begins: incarnating what he knows. "Do this and you will live."

The man responds by continuing the pattern of his schooling. He asks a question that implies there must be a right answer. Instead Jesus tells a story, ending with a question that inverts the lawyer's inquiry. The lawyer asks Jesus, "Who is my neighbor?" (Luke 10:29). But Jesus turns the lawyer's question around, asking, "What do you think? Which of these three was a neighbor to the man?" (Luke 10:36).

Many of this month's lections reveal a similar shift from a religion of right answers to a life of new questions and faithful actions. Responding to those Galatians who are sure that the right answers are to be found in particular religious practices, Paul writes: "All the Law has been fulfilled in a single statement: Love your neighbor as yourself " (Galatians 5:14).

In a similar way, Jesus does not give a list of right answers about how prayer works or what it accomplishes. Instead, he urges us simply to begin praying, trusting that in ways we do not control and cannot predict there will be a response: "Ask and you will receive. Seek and you will find. Knock and the door will be opened to you" (Luke 11:9).

Right answers are great if your mechanic is fixing your car or your physician is reading your test results. But a religion of right answers frequently becomes an attempt to control God. Instead of right answers, Christ offers us the wonder of faith: risking ourselves in prayer and action for the good of our neighbor and the glory of God.

Eat What They Set before You

Year C, Proper 9: Luke 10:1-11, 16-20

When I was a child and our family was invited to eat with neighbors or friends in another part of town, I recall how my mother would give us last-minute instructions on how we were to behave when we arrived. One of the things she always said was that we were to eat whatever was served. Although in our own home our parents might excuse us from eating boiled okra or spinach, when we were guests in another household we were to honor them by eating whatever was served. No refusal. No comment—unless, of course, it was some expression of delight. My mother's command was not always easy to observe, but I remember the telling glance of my mother or my father as something was placed on my plate that looked to me unpalatable. Their focused eyes said as clearly as any sentence they could have pronounced: "Yes, you will eat that. It's better than you think." In fact it sometimes was, but not always! Nevertheless, whether I loved or hated it, I ate it.

All of these memories rush back upon me when I read Jesus' words: "Whenever you enter a city and its people welcome you, eat what they set before you" (Luke 10:8). Something primal is going on in this verse that no preacher can ignore.

Note the first part of it: people who welcome you. What a lovely and gracious reality it is when a congregation welcomes a preacher, when members open their hearts and minds, creating a hospitable space for the preacher's words and insights. But when that happens the preacher must reciprocate their openness and hospitality, gratefully accepting what these people offer.

I think, for example, of a minister I once knew who moved from an urban to a rural parish. He was a gifted preacher, but his urban mind was flummoxed when his rural parishioners would take him into their fields to show him how their crops were doing. It struck him as banal and irrelevant. He did not last long there because he did not eat what they set before him.

Caught in a Squeeze

Year C, Proper 9: Luke 10:1-11, 16-20, Proper 10: Amos 7:7-17

Rush hour. Cars and six-wheelers tailgate each other. Your hands grip the wheel as you try to merge from an entrance ramp. No one gives you room to move into the traffic. The right side of the road closes in as you approach the end of your lane.

Preaching can be like that. Preachers find themselves between two implacable forces, neither one of them giving way to the other. Consider the prophet Amos. He was by his own admission "not a prophet, nor . . . a prophet's son; but . . . a shepherd, and a trimmer of sycamore trees" when the Lord called him, saying: "Go, prophesy to my people Israel" (Amos 7:14-15). Amos responded—and found himself caught in a squeeze between two forces.

One force was the weight of divine judgment upon the economic injustices of the age, the power of a word that demanded to be spoken. The other force was the entrenched establishment that did not want to hear such a word. Amaziah, the court priest, did not tell Amos to stop prophesying, but rather to go back to Judah, to the land he came from and to prophesy there (Amos 7:12-13). If the preacher is called to speak upsetting things, let the preacher do it in another church, but not here in our congregation!

What is a preacher to do? The response can be as urgent and difficult as a driver's decision to hit the brakes or step on the gas. Either way there is the possibility of a crash. If the preacher brakes, if the preacher withholds God's word, there can be an inner crash, a collision between the compunction to be faithful and the desire to keep the peace. If the preacher steps on the gas, if the preacher declares the disturbing truth to those who do not want to be disturbed, then there can be a crash between the establishment and the preacher who tells the brash truth. Perhaps this is why Jesus instructs his disciples to take nothing on their mission trip (Luke 10:4): if they travel light they will be more adroit when caught in the squeeze of countervailing forces.

The Unsupportable Weight of Words

Year C, Proper 10: Amos 7:7-17

Several years ago, when my wife and I wanted to remodel our home, we thought of taking out the wall that stood between the kitchen and the pantry. But when we consulted with the contractor, he explained that it was a load-bearing wall, and the whole back of the house would collapse if we eliminated it. The only solution would be to use a steel I-beam, which turned out to be too costly for our budget.

In ancient oral cultures, words often carried a weight as heavy as the mass of construction that lay upon the load-bearing wall of our kitchen. There was an insupportable materiality to certain words that were spoken in the name of God: "Then Amaziah, the priest of Bethel, sent to King Jeroboam of Israel, saying, 'Amos has conspired against you in the very center of the house of Israel; the land is not able to bear all his words' " (Amos 7:10 NRSV). The words of a prophet were not merely descriptive—they set in motion the events and actions that they announced.

Although to us this may seem a magical and antiquated understanding of language, there is in it, as is often the case with ancient beliefs, a truth that we hide behind our supposedly more sophisticated ways of thinking. For in fact words *can* set off the events they predict. Think of the child who is told, "You will never amount to anything." Or another child who is told, "You can do it. Go ahead and try." Or a nation that hears, "We must have more room for the super race." Or, "I have a dream . . ." For ill and for good words possess power to initiate the realities they announce. That is one reason why we preach: because we believe in the potency of language, its capacity to bear not just our thought but to be a medium of the *logos* of God, the creating and redeeming power of the Holy One who transforms the world.

In the case of Amos, the particular words are devastating. Over and over he speaks against the injustice and religious arrogance of the prosperous Israelites. Amos does not whisper his words of judgment in hidden corners of the realm but speaks them "in the very center of the house of Israel." No wonder the establishment chaplain, Amaziah the priest, is enraged. Amos is delivering words whose weight is too immense for the house of Israel to bear.

The showdown between Amos and Amaziah often replays itself in our ministries. We feel the tension between two frequently conflicted functions of our calling: to maintain the structures of church and society, and to speak words that many people cannot bear, words to set off forces of transformation in church and society.

During this period of Ordinary Time, listen again to the conflict between Amos and Amaziah, especially as you prepare to preach on Independence weekend. Give thanks for freedom, but do not forget all the people who are left out of the promises of the good society. Do not forget them as did the prosperous Israelites, who loved to "lounge on their ivory couches and . . . sing idle songs and . . . drink wine," but were never "grieved over the ruin of Joseph" (Amos 6:4-8 NRSV). Instead, pray as you create your sermon, "God of justice and compassion, do not let Amaziah the priest in me silence Amos the prophet in me."

Credit Card Spirituality

Year C, Proper 13: Luke 12:13-21, Proper 14: Luke 12:32-40

Religion is out. Spirituality is in. At least that is what I read in the papers and journals and hear on the television. *Spirituality* can be an amorphous term, hard to pin down with a precise definition. This does not mean it has no value. Clearly it represents some great hunger that neither our materialist culture nor our established religious traditions are satisfying.

At the risk of oversimplification, I would say that most of the popular articles and books I have perused are interested in a spirituality of the heart: there is a desire for a sense of inward peace, personal wholeness, and harmony with nature. Such values are not inimical to the gospel, and there have been many Christian spiritual disciplines through the centuries that nurtured a religion of the heart that strengthened faith and brought their practitioners these longed for inner qualities.

I would not in the name of Christ attack anyone's search for a deeper sense of spiritual integration. But in this search we must not neglect the passages in the Gospels that suggest any authentic spirituality will attend to how we spend our money: "Where your treasure is, there your heart will be too" (Luke 12:34). Economics interfuses spirituality. If we want to deal with a spirituality of the heart, our credit card statement is a revealing place to begin. It discloses where our hearts in fact reside.

What would happen if we prayed our credit card statement? *O Source of Every Good and Perfect Gift, I lift before you the following expenses.* And then we read aloud to God our last month's expenditures. The goal would be an utterly honest spirituality, one that helped us to understand the true location of our hearts. There would be expenditures for which we would give great thanks: for food that fed the family, for an extravagant gift for a beloved friend, for a contribution that helped a vital cause. But there would also be other expenses revealing where we wished our hearts did not dwell. I wonder how things might have turned out if the rich man who kept building bigger barns (Luke 12:16-21) had practiced credit card spirituality.

Heart to Heart

Year C, Proper 13: Hosea 11:1-11, Proper 15: Isaiah 5:1-7

Oh, the vacillations of love! They begin in early childhood. Some days we exclaim, "Mommy, Daddy, I love you," and other days, "I hate you. I'm running away and never coming back," and still other days, "I'm sorry. I love you, I love you." The range of oscillations in the human heart is immense, and its amplitude and complexity grow with the years.

How do we account for the vacillations of love? One way is to turn to psychology and to consider the interrelationship of internal drives and external forces. Another is to study the biochemical-physiological nature of the human brain and body. As people of faith we are grateful for the light that the social and natural sciences throw upon the processes of our passions, but the sum total of their explanations still lacks something that many of our readings suggest: namely, that the vacillations of human love may reflect a similar dynamic in the heart of our Creator.

Consider, for example, the beginning of Isaiah 5: "Let me sing for my loved one a love song for his vineyard: / My loved one had a vineyard on a fertile hillside" (Isaiah 5:1). If we stop at the end of that first verse, we might expect that what follows will be a romantic ballad, but instead we get a stern judgment against the inhabitants of Judah who have brought forth "bloodshed" instead of "justice," and who have moved God's heart from love to anger: "I'll turn [Jerusalem] into a ruin" (Isaiah 5:6-7).

Perhaps even more dramatic is the vacillation of God's heart in Hosea. The prophet pictures God in a rage, like parents at their wits' end with a stubbornly disobedient child. God is ready to throw them out of the house: "They will return to the land of Egypt, / and Assyria will be their king" (Hosea 11:5), and yet at the last minute God's heart oscillates back to mercy: "My heart winces within me, / my compassion grows warm and tender" (Hosea 11:8).

If God's heart knows the vacillations of love, then who are we to deny them in ourselves? But remember this: in the end God chooses mercy and compassion over anger and rejection, and when we do the same, our hearts give witness to the heart of God.

A Parable Rewritten

Year C, Proper 17: Luke 14:1, 7-14

The football game was over, the stadium crowd streaming back into the parking lot, eager to find their cars and beat the rush home. I had been through this drill many times before. The parking lot rush was usually more brutal than the game we had watched on the field. At least the athletes had to play by the rules. There were referees with whistles to blow and flags to throw and penalties to enforce. But in the parking lot there was no referee, no officer, no attendant.

Three columns of vehicles would have to funnel into a single column to get through the exit gate. I knew all the standard strategies. Drivers back out of their place quickly so others know who is in command. They edge the front of their car right up to the bumper of the car in front so no one will even think of trying to compete with them. They stare down others with intense fierceness. They lean on the horn, then throw up their hands and scowl at the person who is trying to squeeze in front of them: "You bird-brained idiot!" I had seen it so many times before, I just assumed it would be the same as always on this particular night.

Turning on my engine, I waited for the chaos to ensue. The constant stop and go, cars moving by inches, the fumes building up in the air, the rising frustration and anger—all a tribute to the human urge for "the place of honor" (Luke 14:8): first one out of the parking lot! But on this one night, I noticed something I had never seen before. The first three cars alternated one with another so that none of them had to come to a full stop. It was as if they were part of a synchronized driving team. The alternating pattern was repeated by the next three and the next three and the next three . . . It was as if they had all been taught, *when you are driving out of a crowded parking lot, give others room to get in front of you and* "*you will be honored in the presence of all*" (Luke 14:10).

I wish I could report that the next time I went to a game, grace again descended upon the whole lot of us drivers eager to be the first through the exit. But the old pattern returned. A few games later an officer was assigned to the lot. He would let about fifteen cars from one column leave while the other two waited. It cut down on the honking and the gesturing, but we never again got out of there as fast as when we treated each other with grace and hospitality.

Best Memories

Year C, Proper 17: Hebrews 13:1-8, 15-16

I have never been convinced that sermons filled with exhortation are very effective. The imperative voice wears thin quickly. The commands *do this* and *do that* often awaken resistance: "Okay, if you're such an expert, jump in and do it yourself."

Instead of relying on exhortation alone, the author of Hebrews appeals to his readers' best memories. He encourages them to draw upon those memories as a source of energy for filling the moral demands of their faith: "But remember the earlier days, after you saw the light. You stood your ground while you were suffering from an enormous amount of pressure. . . . So don't throw away your confidence—it brings a great reward" (Hebrews 10:32, 35).

Aware of the wobbling faith of his readers, the author encourages them: "Remember your leaders, those who spoke the word of God to you; consider the outcome of their way of life, and imitate their faith" (Hebrews 13:7 NRSV). I read this verse and I immediately begin to think of particular individuals: my mother who read to me aloud from the Bible every morning; Gretchen Farmer, a grade school Sunday school teacher and the first person I saw slowly fade away to the ravages of cancer; and Richard Weld, my high school pastor through whose intellectually brilliant sermons I heard Christ calling me to the ordained ministry. I conjure these people up in my memories and I find myself considering "the outcome of their way of life." I recall the integrity of each one of them: they were not perfect people, but all who knew them sensed their commitment to living the word of God that they spoke. Remembering their witness, I do exactly what Hebrews suggests: I find new strength to maintain my faith and witness.

The next time you begin to flounder in your role as a preacher, "remember your leaders, those who spoke the word of God to you; consider the outcome of their way of life, and imitate their faith." You may do more than renew your energies for preaching; you may also learn how to revitalize the faith of your listeners by drawing upon their best memories.

Learning from the Children of This Age

Year C, Proper 18: Luke 14:25-33, Proper 20: Luke 16:1-13

How do you help people take seriously the ultimate consequences of their daily actions? Who of us thinks of melting glaciers and dying polar bears when we turn on the ignition in our cars? Perhaps now we do since global warming has become a standard item on the news. But for the most part the brightest fires of our thought and feeling are fueled by our own small worlds.

A lot of Jesus' teaching attempts to break the confines of our self-preoccupation and awaken us to the ultimate consequences of how we live day by day. Jesus appeals to the times when human beings are most apt to think about future results: figuring out if we can afford to finance a construction project or calculating the likelihood of bringing a war to a successful conclusion (Luke 14:28-32) or negotiating for economic viability after receiving a pink slip at work (Luke 16:1-9). Jesus observes that in matters such as these "the children of this age are more shrewd in dealing with their own generation than are the children of light" (Luke 16:8 NRSV). Most of us are both "children of this age" and "children of light." We are children of this age to the extent that we live in the world of conflicts and financial calculations that Jesus' parables succinctly describe. At the same time, we are children of light because we want to follow Jesus faithfully. But we are far more sophisticated as children of this age than we are as children of light.

Imagine you are going to put an addition on your house, "build a tower," to use Jesus' words (Luke 14:28). You hire an architect, review the blueprints, get competing bids, check out contractors' references, shop around for the best home loan deals, and consult with knowledgeable friends. Now imagine you are going to help build a *world* that is an environmentally sustainable home, a place that offers justice to all living things. In short, you are going to join in the redemptive processes of the reign of God. Are your energies as wisely engaged there as they would be in planning an addition to your house?

A Trick Question

Year C, Proper 19: Luke 15:1-10, Proper 21: 1 Timothy 6:6-19

What does it take to create life? Sunlight, water, and the animating linkage of molecular structures? Becoming wealthy enough to do whatever we want and to live wherever we desire?

Wait a minute! Who wrote this exam? *Life* means a great many different things: from an amoeba's swelling pseudopod to the beating of our hearts to a winter cruise in the Caribbean, as in the television commercial that pictures a luxury liner passing an island of palm trees and a woman dancing on the deck who exclaims: "Now this is living!"

The question of what it takes to create life and the multiple ways that people define the word *life* are among the recurring themes of the Bible. They emerge in many different guises during this season's readings. The author of 1 Timothy defines God as the one "who gives life to all things" (6:13), but also notes that there are false versions of what constitutes "the life that really is life" (6:19 NRSV), not the least being the illusions that haunt the wealthy or those eagerly trying to become so.

What is "the life that really is life"? Consider how many times a day the media implicitly answer that question as they bombard us with infomercials and stories of the rich and famous to incite our own acquisitiveness. From our earliest childhood we are beguiled with the message that "the life that really is life" is the life we can purchase.

By way of contrast, Luke collects a series of parables in Luke 15 that show people coming alive at the recovery of something precious that they had lost. The vitality and joy that erupt upon finding one stray sheep or a misplaced coin or a runaway child are the true hallmarks of the life that really is life. In living this real life, we rejoice not in what we securely control, but in those moments of grace and delight that take the heart by surprise so that it overflows with extravagant gratitude.

This is the life that really is life: to be filled with astonishment that we creatures of sunlight, water, and molecular processes can taste the goodness and joy of reconciliation with each other and with the one who created us all.

Foolish Every Sunday

Year C, Proper 21: Jeremiah 32:1-3a, 6-15

Given the insane state of the world, who in their right mind would bother to get up and preach Sunday after Sunday? Who would speak of God in a world that either denies there is a God or invokes the name of the divine to exclude or repress or annihilate others? Who would dare to celebrate the beauty of creation when the glaciers are melting, the rain forests are disappearing, and the air in many cities of the earth is unfit to breathe? Who would give witness to the persistence of love and grace amidst the interlocking power systems and the unbridled greed of big money? Who would risk naming publicly some eternal meaning that threads the evolution of life on this tiny watered stone together with the vastness of a cosmos that is nearly 93 billion light-years wide? Who would be fool enough week after week to keep hope alive when violence and death make a daily harvest of innocent lives? Who would be so foolish?

We preachers would!

Why? After all, preaching is foolish, is it not?

Well, yes, if the state of the world is the only reality within range of your visionary powers, preaching is pure foolishness. If that is the case, then preaching makes no sense at all. Give it up. Take Sundays off. Enjoy what you can of life, because the planet is going to choke to death on polluted water and air.

To preach the word of God to this world looks every bit as foolish as it looked for Jeremiah to purchase a field at Anathoth when Jerusalem was under siege. The prophet and everyone else could see, even though the king and his court were in a state of denial, that Jerusalem would fall and be destroyed (Jeremiah 32). But as accurately as Jeremiah saw the state of the world, his visionary powers extended to the word of God and to the hope that "houses, fields, and vineyards will again be bought in this land" (Jeremiah 32:15). When your visionary powers reach like Jeremiah's to the living God, then what looks like foolishness to the world appears as wisdom to the heart and provides power to do far more than we ever imagined we could. So keep being foolish—every Sunday.

From Terror and Banality to Lament and Hope

Year C, Proper 22: Lamentations 3:19-26, Proper 27: Lamentations 1:1-6

First image on the morning news: dead bodies, flames, buildings in rubble. First commercial: cheerful faces and upbeat music to sell some product we do not need. Terror and banality; terror and banality. Because we see this cycle day after day, we become desensitized to the profound sorrow of our world. We do not weep. We accept the juxtaposition of images as the normal course of human events, when in fact it is an electronic artifice, a creation of a technology that disconnects the heart from tears and compassion.

How different it was for our ancient forebears. The weeping prophet—traditionally thought to be Jeremiah, although it probably is not—describes the response to the destruction of the holy city by the Babylonians:

> She weeps bitterly in the night,
> her tears on her cheek.
> None of her lovers comfort her.
> All her friends lied to her;
> they have become her enemies. (Lamentations 1:2)

We think our technology makes us more sophisticated than our "primitive" forebears. Yet they may have been much more sophisticated about grief and sorrow than we are. They had highly developed forms for the expression of sorrow, which simultaneously allowed for the outpouring of tears while providing some disciplined structure to stabilize the shaking heart. Technically called *laments*, such structures are manifest in the form of Hebrew poetry that is used in the book of Lamentations. For example, the opening verses of Lamentations are a form of acrostic poetry, each verse beginning with the successive letter of the Hebrew alphabet.

The literary structure of lament might be interpreted as a way of putting the mourners who read or hear the text in touch with the deeper structure of reality, namely, the God who even in the midst of judgment and grief remains as an eternal source of comfort:

> Certainly the faithful love
> of the LORD hasn't ended;
> certainly God's compassion
> isn't through!
> They are renewed every morning.
> Great is your faithfulness. (Lamentation 3:22-23)

Here then is a counter-cycle to the cycle of terror and banality that dominates the electronic media: lament and hope; lament and hope. It is a cycle that preachers can explore in their sermons to reconnect the human heart to the heart of God, who gives us the gifts of tears and compassion.

Pray for Them?

Year C, Proper 23: Jeremiah 29:1, 4-7

I f I had been one of the exiles torn from my beloved Jerusalem and forced to live in Babylon, I am not sure I would have welcomed Jeremiah's letter. I probably would have still been waking up at night with nightmares fed by memories of the Babylonian invasion and the long forced march to a strange and foreign land. Night and day the unforgettable images and sensations of what I had been through would come unbidden to my mind: the city's walls under siege, the screams of neighbors as soldiers killed them, my eyes filling with tears as I and others were marched out of the devastated capital, the heavy emptiness expanding in my heart as I trudged mile after mile from home toward a place whose very name I detested.

These are not wild imaginings on my part. We know that the survivors of violence often relive the experience again and again. Some years ago I read an article reporting that medical researchers had identified how a single word or image that recalls a trauma may trigger in the body the same biochemical mixture that was released when the experience first occurred. Assuming something like this happened to those exiled to Babylon, imagine how they might have received Jeremiah's letter, instructing them to settle into their captors' land: "Build houses and settle down; cultivate gardens and eat what they produce. . . . Promote the welfare of the city where I have sent you into exile. Pray to the LORD for it" (Jeremiah 29:5, 7a).

The exiles were to pray for the people who gave them their dreams of terror. *Pray for them?* I cannot say that I would have followed Jeremiah's directive. I am not sure that I would have had that much grace under such circumstances. But I know one who does, one who, with the same spirit and in similar words as Jeremiah, teaches us: "Bless those who curse you. Pray for those who mistreat you" (Luke 6:28). My only hope is to seek by faith and prayer the grace I do not possess from the one who does and who freely gives it to all who ask.

The Source of a Preacher's Freedom

Year C, Proper 23: 2 Timothy 2:8-15

The number of things that can fetter a preacher are endless: an impossible schedule of appointments coupled with an equally impossible number of interruptions, a culture that pressures us with an ever-changing succession of fads that challenge our ability to bring a profounder perspective to our congregation's life, media that reduce the complexity and subtlety of great public issues to sound bites, and personal voices of insecurity that corrode our sense of giftedness and inner authority. Perhaps unlike the writer of 2 Timothy we are not literally chained, but psychologically we feel gripped by a constellation of forces that allow minimum freedom to speak the gospel with imagination and passion. Under such circumstances, how do we find the freedom we need to speak an incisive word to God's people?

The writer of 2 Timothy offers us a striking image of the authentic source of a preacher's freedom: "This is the reason I'm suffering to the point that I'm in prison like a common criminal. But God's word cannot be imprisoned" (2 Timothy 2:9). The freedom of preachers is not a function of their circumstances, but a function of the word of God: the ever-creating, enlightening, and redeeming reality that human contrivance can neither constrain nor confine. The word of God is the irrepressible resilience of the divine vitalities that will rise up from the depths of oppression to cry for justice, from the depths of brokenness to begin healing, from the depths of doubt to nurture faith, from the depths of the grave to bring new life.

This word has the capacity to free us from the chains of our impossible schedules, our fad-driven culture, our superficial media, and our inner insecurities. This does not mean the preacher will no longer feel all of those competing pressures, but those pressures will no longer be the determining realities of the preacher's life and ministry. The word of God will put these pressures in perspective, even bringing judgment upon their idolatrous claims for the preacher's constant attention. A preacher grounded and saturated in this word will be free even when in chains.

Each Breath Is Borrowed Air

Year C, Proper 24: Psalm 121, Proper 25: Luke 18:9-14

When I was a child I would sometimes try to hold my breath as long as I possibly could. I would fill my lungs and even my cheeks with air and then start watching the second hand on the clock to see if I could break my last record. I do not recall how long I could last, but of course, every time, never fail, there would come a second when my closed lips would pop open and the stale air would rush out of me and I would gulp in a refreshing new breath.

As a child, I lacked a scientific understanding of this phenomenon. Instead, I experienced it as something over which I had no control. It seemed to me as if someone else were breathing the old air out and breathing the new air in. Although I would not have had the cognitive sophistication to say so when I was a small child, I look back now and understand that my experience of breath as a gift is very close to that of the ancient Hebrews: God "breathed into [Adam's] nostrils the breath of life" (Genesis 2:7 NRSV).

When we know that each breath is borrowed air, then our primary response to being a living creature is gratitude. Every breath is a gift, and every breath is an offering returned to God.

When we lose our sense of wonder at the marvel of breath, then the posture of our souls turns from gratitude to presumption and forgetfulness, a theme in this month's lections. We assume that we deserve to exist—that it's a right rather than a grace—and forget that we had absolutely nothing to do with our creation. Our ingratitude turns to an inflated self-importance, and self-importance to moral arrogance: "God, I thank you that I'm not like everyone else" (Luke 18:11).

We are in truth the same as all other people: we are breathing beings utterly and entirely dependent upon the one who creates and sustains us. "My help [and my very being] comes from the LORD, / the maker of heaven and earth" (Psalm 121:2). When we recognize this elemental fact of existence along with the psalmist, then we understand that humility belongs to the very nature of being a creature: "For all who exalt themselves will be humbled, but all who humble themselves will be exalted" (Luke 18:14 NRSV). To know this is to sing with all that we are:

Each breath is borrowed air,
not ours to keep and own,
and all our breaths as one declare
what wisdom long has known:
to live is to receive
and answer back with praise
to what our minds cannot conceive
the source of all our days.[3]

No Installment Plan Required

Year C, Proper 26: Luke 19:1-10, Reign of Christ: Luke 23:33-43

On *sale today and today only! Easy installment plan!* I do not know how many times I have heard or seen that advertising come-on. It is often for big-ticket items such as major household appliances. Sometimes you get a good deal. But even if you pay less than you usually would, the bill is still going to come due when the charge card statement arrives or as the installments stretch out over the coming years. It sounds as though you buy it today and the sale is complete. But in fact the "today-ness" is an illusion. It is a today encumbered with the weight of many tomorrows.

That alluring word *today* appears at least twice in the Gospel readings for this month. Jesus tells Zacchaeus, "Today, salvation has come to this household" (Luke 19:9), and just before the crucifixion Jesus responds to the criminal who asks to be remembered: "I assure you that today you will be with me in paradise" (Luke 23:43). Today, salvation! Today, paradise! Christ's *today* is a genuine today. It is not a today that is encumbered with the weight of many tomorrows. Yes, of course, there are the profound issues of the cost of discipleship for Zacchaeus, and there is sorrow that the criminal waited to the last minute for anything resembling repentance. But none of that erases the accessibility, the hospitality, the receptivity, the acceptance, the embrace, and the utter graciousness of Jesus. They are available today. No installment plan is required.

Of all the realities that Christ revealed, I believe none is more difficult for us to believe and accept with the fullness of our being than the grace that freely and abundantly flows from the heart of God. Perhaps our consumer culture with all of its economic encumbrances reinforces the human propensity to reject grace—but the witness of history suggests the resistance lies in our very character.

It would be salutary for all preachers to start with themselves and examine their own resistance. Imagine if every time we preached, our heart and the hearts of our congregation finally realized: Today, salvation! Today, paradise! No installment plan required.

Speaking Different Languages

Year C, Proper 26: Luke 19:1-10, Proper 28: Luke 21:5-19,
Reign of Christ: Luke 23:33-43

Sometimes when we cannot get another person to understand us, we exclaim in frustration: "You and I do not speak the same language!" We may both be speaking English and even use the same accent and colloquialisms, but the different ways we perceive, process, and interpret reality are at odds with each other. "You and I do not speak the same language."

The conflict of different languages is apparent in several of the readings for this month. Jesus speaks the language of grace and acceptance to an outcast tax collector: "Zacchaeus, come down at once. I must stay in your home today" (Luke 19:5). But the crowd speaks a completely different language, an idiom of judgment that cannot comprehend the idiom of grace: "Everyone who saw this grumbled, saying, 'He has gone to be the guest of a sinner'" (Luke 19:7). At the crucifixion, one thief speaks the taunting and damning language of the mob: "Aren't you the Christ? Save yourself and us!" (Luke 23:39). But the other thief has found the language of trust and prayer: "Jesus, remember me when you come into your kingdom" (Luke 23:42).

The Gospels portray all the characters speaking in Greek, but they do not speak the same language. Jesus even warns the disciples that the language he gives them is a language that the powers of this world cannot comprehend: "I'll give you words and a wisdom that none of your opponents will be able to counter or contradict" (Luke 21:15).

Jesus and the world do not speak the same language. Jesus speaks grace; the world speaks keeping track of every wrong. Jesus speaks pouring oneself out in love; the world speaks brutal force. Herein lies the greatest communications quandary that Christian preachers face: how do we break through to a world that speaks a different language?

The answer lies in the seasons of Advent and Christmas that are before us. We are to prepare for the Word that is more than words. We are to pattern our own lives after the Word made flesh: incarnating the meaning of God's language in acts of love and justice.

Temple Views

Year C, Proper 27: Haggai 1:15b–2:9, Proper 28: Luke 21:5-19

Sometimes the lectionary provides within the span of a single week two very different perspectives on the same image or theme. Consider Haggai urging the reconstruction of the temple after the repatriation of the exiles to Jerusalem, and then the next week's lection, in which Christ prophesies the destruction of the temple. More than five centuries separate the two passages that offer such distinctly different views on the significance of the temple. Read in tandem, they give witness to both the necessity and the danger of building a sacred place to the glory of God.

Haggai considered the reconstruction of the temple an urgent necessity, claiming its completion would usher in a new age of prosperity and prestige. Whether or not we agree with the prophet's theology, there is something affecting in his appeal to the storied past of the temple:

> Who among you is left who saw
> this house in its former glory?
> How does it look to you now?
> Doesn't it appear as nothing to you? (Haggai 2:3)

My study Bible indicates that someone "would have to have been at least seventy-three years of age when Haggai said these words" in order to remember that former glory.[4] A span of time that long plays a lot of tricks with the memory. If there were any people present in Haggai's day who remembered the former temple, it might well have appeared in their mind's eye more glorious than it had been in actuality, its munificence amplified by contrast with the ruins. I can almost hear an elderly voice reminiscing, "Oh, yes, I remember, I remember the temple and how grand it was when I was a child." Perhaps such memories spurred on the younger workers who responded to the prophet's call.

Haggai reminds us that there is something in the human soul that craves a sacred space, while Matthew warns us that, as impressive as sacred space may be, no temple built by human hands will stand forever. The two passages side by side provide a theology about the structures that organized religion builds: they meet the human need for tangible expression of what is holy and ineffable, but they are not to be confused with the eternal spirit of the living God.

A Message Not Paid for by Any Candidate

Year C, Proper 28: Isaiah 65:17-25

I know I am not the only one who is exhausted and frustrated by the political life of our nation. I find my energy for serious engagement with the issues enervated by the charges and countercharges, the negativity, the use of the flag to suggest one side is more patriotic than the other, the amalgamation of slick images and music to turn a candidate into a heroic figure whose subliminal appeal may snag the vote of the unwary viewer. What can preachers do in such an acrimonious and manipulative environment to lift the character of our political debate to a more substantive level of discussion?

There are some pulpits where preachers are free to come out squarely for one candidate or another. The danger in this is that politics is always a conglomeration of conflicting interests, and using the name of God to bless one candidate over another easily leads to demagoguery or to the distortions of moralism—good versus evil—when in fact things are not that simple.

There are other pulpits where the congregation would consider it an abuse of homiletical privilege if the preacher sided with one candidate or party. The danger in this is that the pulpit may fall silent when people need to hear some illuminating word about the social and moral issues that are interwoven with our politics.

Isaiah 65:17-25 provides an alternative to favoring one candidate over another and an alternative to remaining silent. The prophet announces a vision of the new heaven and the new earth that God is going to create, vividly describing the kind of society that God intends for human beings: a society at peace where people live long, healthy, and productive lives. It may seem elementary and even naïve to declare such a vision in the midst of the political rancor that marks these current days. But it is precisely when people get lost in their own political shortsightedness that they most need to be reminded of the fundamental social values that spring from the heart of our just and compassionate God.

Transubstantiation in a New Light

Year C, Thanksgiving: John 6:24-35

Many years ago a physician told me about an article he had read on how food is metabolized to sustain the body, blood, and bone of our material being. We sit down to a plate of cheese and fruit, and our skeleton is strengthened and our soft tissue replenished. The physician told me that the author of the article had used the word *transubstantiation* to describe this biological process. I have no intention of reawakening theological debates about the transubstantiation of the elements in the celebration of the Mass, but I continue to be haunted by the use of the word to describe how food is metabolized into body, blood, and bone. It haunts me because no matter how I may theologically understand the sacrament of Communion, the doctor's use of the word awakens wonder and gratitude at the daily transubstantiation of food into the cells and processes of physical life.

That sense of wonder and gratitude only increases when I consider the transubstantiation of "the bread of God" that "comes down from heaven and gives life to the world" (John 6:33). How does that happen? We cannot examine spiritual processes with the chemical and ocular precision of the scientist tracing cellular transformations through a microscope and laboratory experiments. But here is what I have observed as a priest and minister day in and day out, year after year: when we regularly participate in a community that feeds upon Christ in its worship and prayer, in its mutual support and outward mission, then Christ is transubstantiated into a mode of human existence that blends together faith, compassion, justice, and hope. Their fusioned energies create in us a vital resilience, the very thing John calls eternal life. We remain creatures of dust, but at the same time within and among us there is a quality of being and doing that participates in the never-ending life and love of God.

If a human body is denied food, then it feeds upon itself and the result is emaciation and eventually death. If we do not feed on Christ, we devour ourselves. But if we do, then the bread from heaven gives life through us to the world.

NOTES

Year A

1. Thomas H. Troeger, "Our Savior's Infant Cries Were Heard," in *Borrowed Light: Hymn Texts, Prayers and Poems* (New York: Oxford University Press, 1994), 92.
2. *The Psalter: A faithful and inclusive rendering from the Hebrew into contemporary English poetry, intended primarily for communal song and recitation* (Chicago: Liturgy Training Publications, 1994).
3. Robert Alter, *The Book of Psalms: A Translation with Commentary* (New York: W. W. Norton & Company, 2007), 142.
4. Michael Benson, *Far Out: A Space-Time Chronicle* (New York: Abrams, 2009).
5. Ibid., 11.
6. Ibid., 7.
7. Ibid., 10.
8. Ibid., 9.
9. The full text is available at http://www.mircea-eliade.com/from-primitives-to-zen/132.html.
10. Quoted in the footnote on 1 Thessalonians 4:13 in *The HarperCollins Study Bible*, ed. Wayne A. Meeks (New York: HarperCollins, 1993), NRSV, 2223.

Year B

1. I am indebted to my colleague Don Messer, who once preached a sermon "A Conspiracy of Goodness," which he later developed into a book, *A Conspiracy of Goodness: Contemporary Images of Christian Mission* (Nashville: Abingdon Press, 1992).

Year C

1. Carroll Stuhlmueller, C. P., "Deutero-Isaiah," in *The Jerome Biblical Commentary Vol. 1*, ed. Raymond E. Brown, S. S. , Joseph A. Fitzmyer, S. J., Roland E. Murphy, O. Carm. (Englewood Cliffs, New Jersey: Prentice Hall, 1968), 383.
2. Othmar Keel, *The Symbolism of the Biblical World* (New York: Seabury Press, 1978), 354.
3. Thomas H. Troeger, *Above the Moon Earth Rises: hymn texts, anthems and poems for a new creation* (New York: Oxford University Press, 2001), 8.
4. Wayne A. Meeks, ed., *The HarperCollins Study Bible* (New York: HarperCollins, 1993), NRSV, 1409.

INDEX BY BIBLICAL PASSAGE

If a biblical passage listed in The Common Lectionary is missing from the index, there is no homiletical reflection on it in this book.

Genesis 1-2:4a, pp. 27-28, 28-29
Genesis 2:15-17; 3:1-7, pp. 17-18
Genesis 9:8-17, pp. 53-54
Genesis 15:1-12, 17-18, pp. 100-01

Exodus 20:1-17, pp. 53-54
Exodus 24:12-18, pp. 16-17
Exodus 34:29-35, pp. 98-99

Deuteronomy 11:18-21, 26-28, pp. 33-34
Deuteronomy 26:1-11, pp. 97-98

2 Kings 5:1-14, pp. 51-52, 52-53

Job 38:1-11, pp. 64-65

Psalm 8, p. 30
Psalm 23, pp. 22-23
Psalm 27, pp. 101-2
Psalm 40:1-11, pp. 14-15
Psalm 91:1-2, 9-16, pp. 99-100
Psalm 104:1-9, 24, 35c, pp. 78-79
Psalm 121, pp. 130-31

Isaiah 5:1-7, pp. 120-21
Isaiah 11:1-10, pp. 5-6
Isaiah 35:1-10, pp. 6-7, 7-8
Isaiah 40:1-11, pp. 47-48
Isaiah 42:1-9, pp. 13-14
Isaiah 43:16-21, pp. 106-7
Isaiah 43:18-25, pp. 51-52, 52-53
Isaiah 60:1-6, pp. 12-13
Isaiah 62:1-5, pp. 95-96
Isaiah 63:7-9, pp. 6-7
Isaiah 64:1-9, pp. 47-48
Isaiah 65:17-25, pp. 134-35

Jeremiah 17:5-10, pp. 98-99
Jeremiah 29:1, 4-7, p. 128
Jeremiah 32:1-3a, 6-15, pp. 125-26

Lamentations 1:1-6, pp. 126-27
Lamentations 3:19-26, pp. 126-27

Ezekiel 37:1-14, pp. 19-20

Hosea 11:1-11, pp. 120-21

Joel 2:21-27, pp. 85-86

Amos 7:7-17, pp. 117-18, 118-19

Haggai 1:15b–2:9, pp. 133-34

Matthew 1:18-25, pp. 6-7
Matthew 2:1-12, pp. 11, 12-13
Matthew 2:13-23, pp. 5-6, 7-8
Matthew 3:1-12, pp. 6-7
Matthew 4:1-11, pp. 16-17
Matthew 4:12-23, pp. 13-14
Matthew 6:25-33, pp. 86-87
Matthew 7:21-29, pp. 15-16
Matthew 9:9-13, 18-26, pp. 34-35
Matthew 11:2-11, pp. 5-6
Matthew 11:16-19, 25-30, p. 36
Matthew 13:1-9, 18-23, p. 37
Matthew 13:24-30, 36-43, p. 37
Matthew 13:31-33, 44-52, p. 37
Matthew 14:13-21, p. 38
Matthew 14:22-33, pp. 38, 39
Matthew 16:13-20, p. 39
Matthew 16:21-28, p. 40
Matthew 18:15-20, pp. 40, 41

Matthew 18:21-35, pp. 40, 41
Matthew 22:15-22, p. 43
Matthew 22:34-46, pp. 42, 43
Matthew 23:1-12, p. 44
Matthew 25:1-13, p. 45
Matthew 25:14-30, pp. 44, 45
Matthew 25:31-46, p. 45

Mark 1:14-20, pp. 49-50
Mark 1:21-28, pp. 50-51, 51-52
Mark 4:35-41, pp. 62, 63-64
Mark 5:21-43, pp. 65-66
Mark 6:14-29, pp. 67-68
Mark 7:1-8, 14-15, 21-23, pp. 72-73, 73-74
Mark 7:24-37, pp. 73-74
Mark 8:27-38, pp. 73-74, 74-75
Mark 8:31-38, pp. 53-54
Mark 9:2-9, pp. 53-54
Mark 9:30-38, pp. 73-74, 74-75
Mark 9:38-50, pp. 75-76
Mark 10:2-16, pp. 76-77, 77-78
Mark 10:17-31, pp. 77-78
Mark 10:35-45, pp. 76-77, 77-78
Mark 10:46-52, pp. 77-78
Mark 12:28-34, pp. 79-81, 81-82
Mark 12:38-44, pp. 81-82
Mark 15:1-39 (40-47), pp. 55-56
Mark 16:1-8, pp. 57-58

Luke 1:39-45, pp. 90-91, 91-92
Luke 3:1-6, pp. 90-91
Luke 3:7-18, pp. 91-92
Luke 3:15-17, 21-22, pp. 93-94, 94-95
Luke 4:1-13, pp. 99-100
Luke 4:14-21, pp. 94-95, 96-97
Luke 4:21-30, pp. 94-95
Luke 5:1-11, pp. 97-98
Luke 6:17-26, pp. 97-98
Luke 6:27-38, pp. 98-99
Luke 7:36–8:3, pp. 111-12
Luke 8:26-39, pp. 111-12, 113-14
Luke 9:51-62, pp. 114-115
Luke 10:1-11, 16-20, pp. 116-17, 117-18
Luke 10:25-37, pp. 114-15, 115-16
Luke 11:1-13, pp. 115-16
Luke 12:13-21, pp. 119-20

Luke 12:32-40, pp. 119-20
Luke 13:31-35, pp. 102-3
Luke 14:1, 7-14, pp. 121-22
Luke 14:25-33, pp. 123-24
Luke 15:1-10, pp. 124-25
Luke 15:1-3, 11b-32, pp. 102-3, 104
Luke 16:1-13, pp. 123-24
Luke 18:9-14, pp. 130-31
Luke 19:1-10, pp. 131-32, 132-33
Luke 21:5-19, pp. 132-33, 133-34
Luke 23:1-49, pp. 105, 106-7
Luke 23:33-34, pp. 131-32, 132-33
Luke 24:1-12, pp. 106-107
Luke 24:13-35, pp. 25-26, 26-27
Luke 24:13-49, pp. 56-57
Luke 24:36b-48, pp. 58-59

John 1:1-14, pp. 9, 47-48, 48-49, 92-93
John 2:1-11, pp. 94-95
John 3:1-17, p. 61
John 3:14-21, pp. 54-55
John 4:5-42, pp. 19-20
John 6:1-21, p. 69
John 6:24-35, pp. 135-36
John 6:35, 41-51, pp. 70-71
John 7:37-39, pp. 28-29
John 10:1-10, pp. 25-26
John 10:11-18, p. 60
John 10:22-30, pp. 108-9
John 13:31-35, pp. 108-9
John 14:1-14, pp. 26-27
John 14:15-21, pp. 27-28
John 14:23-29, pp. 108-109
John 15:1-8, pp. 56-57
John 16:12-15, pp. 111-12, 112-13
John 17:1-11, pp. 28-29
John 17:20-26, pp. 108-9, 110-11
John 18:1-19–19:42, pp. 21-22
John 18:33-37, pp. 82-83, 83-84
John 20:1-18, pp. 19-20, 22-23, 23-24
John 20:19-23, pp. 27-28
John 20:19-31, pp. 23-24, 24-25, 106-7
John 21:1-19, pp. 106-7

Acts 1:1-11, pp. 56-57
Acts 1:6-14, pp. 27-28
Acts 2:1-21, pp. 29-30

Acts 8:26-40, pp. 58-59
Acts 16:16-34, pp. 109-10

Romans 5:1-8, p. 35
Romans 8:26-39, p. 36
Romans 11:1-2a, 29-32, p. 39

1 Corinthians 12:12-31a, pp. 93-94
1 Corinthians 13:1-13, pp. 97-98
1 Corinthians 15:1-11, pp. 98-99
1 Corinthians 15:19-26, pp. 107-8

2 Corinthians 12:2-10, pp. 66-67

Galatians 5:1, 13-25, pp. 115-16

Ephesians 1:3-14, pp. 68-69
Ephesians 3:1-12, pp. 12-13
Ephesians 3:14-21, pp. 65-66
Ephesians 4:25–5:2, pp. 70-71

Philippians 1:3-11, pp. 89-90
Philippians 2:5-11, pp. 19-20, 20-21
Philippians 4:1-9, p. 42

1 Thessalonians 3:9-13, pp. 89-90
1 Thessalonians 4:13-18, p. 44

1 Timothy 6:6-19, pp. 124-25

2 Timothy 2:8-15, p. 129

Hebrews 1:1-4; 2:5-12, pp. 64-65
Hebrews 2:10-18, p. 10
Hebrews 4:12-16, pp. 76-77
Hebrews 13:1-8, 15-16, pp. 122-23

James 1:17-27, pp. 71-72
James 3:1-12, pp. 72-73

Revelation 1:4b-8, pp. 81-82, 84-85
Revelation 7:9-17, pp. 109-10
Revelation 21:1-6, pp. 109-10

INDEX BY
LITURGICAL SEASON

The index is organized by the order of the liturgical seasons rather than alphabetically. If a Sunday or Holy day is missing from this index, either there is no homiletical reflection on it in this book or it appears under another liturgical year since the lectionary repeats several passages every year. If you do not find the lection you are looking for here, see if it is listed in the Index by Biblical Passage.

Year A

Advent 2, pp. 5-6, 6-7
Advent 3, pp. 5-7, 6-7, 7-8
Advent 4, pp. 6-7
Christmas Day, p. 9
Christmas 1 (First Sunday after Christmas), pp. 7-8, 10
Epiphany, pp. 11, 12-13
Epiphany 1, pp. 13-14
Epiphany 2, pp. 14-15
Epiphany 3, pp. 13-14
Epiphany 9, pp. 15-16
Transfiguration (Sunday before Ash Wednesday), pp. 16-17
Lent 1, pp. 16-17, 17-18
Lent 3, pp. 19-20
Lent 4, p. 18
Lent 5, pp. 19-20
Palm/Passion Sunday, pp. 19-20, 20-21
Good Friday, pp. 21-22
Easter 1 (Easter Day), pp. 19-20, 22-23, 23-24
Easter 2, pp. 23-24, 24-25
Easter 3, pp. 25-26, 26-27
Easter 4, pp. 25-26
Easter 5, pp. 26-27
Easter 6, pp. 27-28
Easter 7, pp. 27-28, 28-29
Pentecost, pp. 27-28, 28-29, 30-31
Trinity Sunday, pp. 27-28, 28-29, 30-31

Ordinary Time, a general reflection on the season, pp. 31-32
Proper 4, pp. 33-34
Proper 5, pp. 34-35
Proper 6, p. 35
Proper 9, p. 36
Proper 10, p. 37
Proper 11, p. 37
Proper 12, pp. 36, 37
Proper 13, p. 38
Proper 14, pp. 38, 39
Proper 15, p. 39
Proper 16, p. 39
Proper 17, p. 40
Proper 18, pp. 40, 41
Proper 19, pp. 40, 41
Proper 23, p. 42
Proper 24, p. 43
Proper 25, pp. 42, 43
Proper 26, p. 44
Proper 27, pp. 44, 45
Proper 28, pp. 44, 45
Reign of Christ, p. 45

Year B

Advent 1, pp. 47-48
Advent 2, pp. 47-48
Christmas Day, pp. 47-48, 48-49
Epiphany 3, pp. 49-50
Epiphany 4, pp. 50-51, 51-52
Epiphany 6, pp. 51-52, 52-53

Epiphany 7, pp. 51-52, 52-53
Transfiguration (Sunday before Ash Wednesday), pp. 53-54
Lent 1, pp. 53-54
Lent 2, pp. 53-54
Lent 3, pp. 53-54
Lent 4, pp. 54-55
Palm/Passion Sunday, pp. 55-56
Easter Eve, pp. 56-57
Easter 1 (Easter Day), pp. 57-58
Easter 3, pp. 58-59
Easter 4, p. 60
Easter 5, pp. 56-57, 58-59
Ascension, pp. 56-57
Trinity Sunday, p. 61
Proper 7, pp. 62, 63-64, 64-65
Proper 8, pp. 65-66
Proper 9, pp. 66-67
Proper 10, pp. 67-68, 68-69
Proper 12, pp. 65-66, 69
Proper 14, pp. 70-71
Proper 17, pp. 71-72, 72-73, 73-74
Proper 18, pp. 73-74
Proper 19, pp. 72-73, 73-74, 74-75
Proper 20, pp. 73-74, 74-75
Proper 21, pp. 75-76
Proper 22, pp. 64-65, 76-77, 77-78
Proper 23, pp. 76-77, 77-78
Proper 24, pp. 76-77, 77-78, 78-79
Proper 25, pp. 77-78
Proper 26, pp. 79-81, 81-82
Proper 27, pp. 81-82
Reign of Christ, pp. 81-82, 82-83, 83-84, 84-85
Thanksgiving, pp. 85-86, 86-87

Year C

Advent 1, pp. 89-90
Advent 2, pp. 89-90, 90-91
Advent 3, pp. 91-92
Advent 4, pp. 90-91, 91-92
Christmas Day, pp. 92-93
Epiphany 1, pp. 93-94, 94-95
Epiphany 2, pp. 94-95, 95-96

Epiphany 3, pp. 93-94, 94-95, 96-97
Epiphany 4, pp. 94-95, 97-98
Epiphany 5, pp. 97-98, 98-99
Epiphany 6, pp. 97-98, 98-99
Epiphany 7, pp. 98-99
Transfiguration (Sunday before Ash Wednesday), pp. 98-99
Lent 1, pp. 97-98, 99-100
Lent 2, pp. 100-01, 101-2, 102-3
Lent 4, pp. 102-3, 104-5
Lent 5, pp. 106-7
Palm/Passion Sunday, pp. 105, 106-7
Easter Vigil, pp. 106-7
Easter 1 (Easter Day), pp. 107-8
Easter 2, pp. 106-7
Easter 3, pp. 106-7
Easter 4, pp. 108-9, 109-10
Easter 5, pp. 108-9, 109-10
Easter 6, pp. 108-9
Easter 7, pp. 108-9, 109-10, 110-11
Trinity Sunday, pp. 111-12, 112-13
Proper 6, pp. 111-12
Proper 7, pp. 111-12, 113-14
Proper 8, pp. 114-15, 115-16
Proper 9, pp. 116-17, 117-18
Proper 10, pp. 114-15, 115-16, 117-18, 118-19
Proper 13, pp. 119-20, 120-21
Proper 14, pp. 119-20
Proper 15, pp. 120-21
Proper 17, pp. 121-22, 122-23
Proper 18, pp. 123-24
Proper 19, pp. 124-25
Proper 20, pp. 123-24
Proper 21, pp. 124-25, 125-26
Proper 22, pp. 126-27
Proper 23, pp. 128, 129
Proper 24, pp. 130-31
Proper 25, pp. 130-31
Proper 26, pp. 131-32, 132-33
Proper 27, pp. 126-27, 133-34
Proper 28, pp. 132-33, 134-35
Reign of Christ, pp. 132-33
Thanksgiving, pp. 135-36

INDEX BY THEME,
IMAGE, AND
PASTORAL NEED

absolutism, how to deal with theological commandants, 43
ambiguities
in the Bible, 95-96
in ministry, 94-95
angels, 10

bad guys, redeemed by Christ the good guy, 34-35
belonging to Christ, 83-84
Bible, pointing beyond itself to the Spirit, 112-13
blood and water, 21-22
body of Christ
connective tissue of the Spirit, 93-94
feeding on, to sustain life of the church, 135-36
breath
as borrowed air, as a gift, 130-31
unfailing spirit of God, 27-28

change
possibility of, through Christ, 20-21
chaos monster
confronted by reign of God, 28-29
Christ
as good guy redeeming the bad guy, 34-35
presence of, here and now, forever, 108-9
Christmas
Christmas cards featuring words from Advent lessons, 6-7
circles of exclusion and inclusion, 12-13
conspiracy of goodness
mystery of God's will and grace, 68

cosmology,
God's love for the earth as a miniscule mote, 30-31
the surprising significance of a generous act, 81-82
cross
bearing it as a choice not a compulsion, 55-56

death and dying
childhood memories of the Twenty-third Psalm, 18

ears
dug out by God, 14-15
having ears to hear a parable, 104
Easter. See resurrection
eschatology
changing the here and now, 45
starting at the end to empower the present, 31-33
experience and trust, in the life of faith, 66-67
extravagance of God, 47

faith, God's faith in us, 39
forgiveness, complex relationship to judgment, 40

genie in a bottle spirituality, 16-17
God, astounding range of relationship to, 64-65
good news, shaken by it, 49-50
grace
as a conspiracy of goodness, 68
different from an automated phone system, 35

grace, *continued*
  empowering us to live the com-
    mandments of Christ, 86-87
  experienced in a stadium parking
    lot, 121-22
  inefficient character of, 60
  as a language different from the
    world's, 132-33
  offered today, no installment plan,
    131-32
grief, reframed by resurrection, 44

harmony, as metaphor for living in the
    Spirit, 36
healing, resisted, 113-14
hearing
  Bible stories through the ears of the
    early church, 63-64
  of people listening to preachers, 67-
    68
  restored, 14-15
heart
  clearing out the cluttered heart, 91-
    92
  getting the spiritual heart in shape,
    70-71
  optometry for the heart's vision, 78-
    79
  resistance of, to facing the truth of
    suffering, 74-75
  vacillations of the human and the
    divine heart, 120-21
Herod, perplexed by Christ, 82-83
hockey dad story, 40
hope
  fed by the resurrection, 44
  relationship to suffering, 101-2

incarnation
  God's becoming vulnerable to
    human terror, 48-49
  making the world secure through
    grace, 7-8
  as perplexity to worldly power, 82-83
  as the reverse of humans' wants, 76-
    77
inclusivity of the gospel, 12-13

John the Baptist, Christ's reaction to
    his beheading, 38
judgment and grace, balance of, 41

lament, as antidote to artifice of the
    media, 126-27
law, grace of, 33-34
life, conflicting understandings of,
    124-25
love
  amidst church conflict, 97-98
  interrelationship of divine and
    human love, 11

memories, strengthening faith, 122-23
ministry, ambiguities of, 94-95

Nicodemus and woman at the well, 61

paradigm shifts, 51-52
pardon and punishment in Matthew,
    40
Pentecost, Paul's return to Jerusalem,
    29-30
power
  as function of Christ's relationship
    to God, 69
  as gift of wonder and grace, 65-66
prayer
  for enemies, 128
  essential role of, in Christ's life, 38
  importance of, for others, 62
  living the prayers we pray, 99-100
preaching
  authority of, in a suspicious age, 50-
    51
  birthed from action, 75-76
  amidst church conflict, 97-98
  in the congregation's world, 116-17
  doing no harm, 13-14
  as foolishness, 125-26
  function of, 9
  inspiration of, 110
  integrity of, 15-16
  significance of, 90-91
  truth as ultimate criterion of, 72-73

priorities
  living the first commandments, 79-81
  setting before speeding up, 42
prophets
pressures of, 117-18
  weight of the words of, 118-19

rainbow, as sign of a critical question to humanity, 53-54
realism
  biblical realism about humanity, 102-3
  redefined by Advent and Christmas, 5-6
  as revealed through terrifying darkness, 100-01
  about the world and the reign of God, 123-24
reasonable actions
redefined by Christ, 54-55
reign of God,
  our view of, 77-78
  social values of, 134-35
  as top priority, 28-29
religion
  need for tangible expression of the holy, 133-34
  problems with a religion of right answers, 115-16
  relationship to spirituality in Christ's life, 96-97
resistance
  futility of resisting God, 106-7
  to healing, 113-14
resurrection
  delayed recognition of, 23-24
  reframed by grief, 44
  "signs" of Christ's presence in a congregation, 25-26
  speaking to primal fear of death, 107-8
  terror and joy of, 57-58
  unlimited by the season, 22-23
  as a way of interpreting the Bible, 58-59

revelation, what is hidden and what is seen, 105
rush hour, traffic as image for pressures on the preacher, 117-18

sacraments, interrelationship of baptism and communion, 21-22
security, 7-8
shrub, as image of disconnection from God, 98-99
Spirit
  living in harmony with, 36
  relationship to the Bible, 112-13
  speaking to the church, 84-85
  as unfailing breath of God, 27-28
  as unstoppable underground stream, 106-7
  waiting and acting as two approaches to, 56-57
spirituality
  and contrast of biblical and contemporary, 16-17
  relationship to our credit card statement, 119-20
  relationship to religion in Christ's life, 96-97
  starting assumptions, as changed by Christ, 19-20
stereotypes, as overcomed by Christ, 114-15
stream, as image of the Spirit, 106-7
suffering, related to hope, 101-2
suspicious quality of our age, 50-51

taboos, Christ as maker and breaker of, 73-74
talking snake, 17-18
temple, positive and negative aspects of sacred space, 133-34
tenderness, 13-14
thankfulness
  breaking through our reluctance toward, 71-72
  for breath itself, 130-31
  for elements and animals, 85-86
  hungering for, 89-90

transubstantiation, as biophysical
process illuminating feeding on
Christ, 135-36

tree
as image of our connection to God,
98-99
as metaphor for persistent faith, 109-10
trust and experience, 66-67
truth
giving witness to, 92-93
too heavy to bear, 111-12

woman at the well and Nicodemus,
61
word of God
amidst a flood of words, 37
freedom of, even when chained,
129
fullness and variety of ways known,
61
significance of every word, 61
weight of, 118-19